HAMLET'S PERFECTION

Hamlet's Perfection

WILLIAM KERRIGAN

THE JOHNS HOPKINS UNIVERSITY PRESS
BALTIMORE AND LONDON

© 1994 The Johns Hopkins University Press
All rights reserved
Printed in the United States of America on acid-free paper

The Johns Hopkins University Press
2715 North Charles Street
Baltimore, Maryland 21218-4319
The Johns Hopkins Press Ltd., London

Johns Hopkins Paperbacks edition, 1996
05 04 03 02 01 00 99 98 97 96   5 4 3 2 1

LIBRARY OF CONGRESS CATALOGING-IN-PUBLICATION DATA
Kerrigan, William, 1943–
    Hamlet's perfection / William Kerrigan.
          p.   cm.
    Includes bibliographical references (p.) and index.
    ISBN 0-8018-4719-2 (alk. paper)   ISBN 0-8018-5468-7 (pbk.: alk. paper)
    1. Shakespeare, William, 1564-1616. Hamlet.   2. Perfection in
literature.   I. Title.
PR2807.K46   1994
822.3´3—dc20   93-20717

A catalog record for this book is available from the British Library.

FOR CHRISTOPHER, BRIAN, AND ANN

Contents

Preface

None of my books has come to me so quickly and with such conviction as this one. Fate, evening things up, did land some blows toward the end of my labors. Midway through the first draft of this introduction, I was interrupted by the explosion of my water heater. Four hours of panicked bailing no doubt contributed to the tendonitis that inhabited both of my elbows, making even typing—especially typing—a chore. Long hours at the keyboard, sublimely indifferent to the numbness in my legs, probably resulted in the alarming but temporary paralysis of my right foot. But this book is largely the product of a very good mood.

It did, however, take a while to realize exactly what was being visited on me. For reasons discussed in Chapter 1, I had been reading a great deal of *Hamlet* criticism and, in the winter of 1992, at the urging of Edward Tayler, decided to write about it. I sent copies of a draft called "*Hamlet* in History" to my most trusted correspondents, asking them where I might publish this idiosyncratic and unfashionable essay. Within a week I saw the folly of my request: this was not an essay at all, but the first chapter of an idiosyncratic and unfashionable book. It was not fair to excoriate my contemporaries for losing touch with the history of Shakespeare studies without trying to demonstrate in work of my own that this tradition might still inspire fruitful approaches to the play. I could not in good conscience write "*Hamlet* in History" without writing *Hamlet's Perfection*.

Horace Howard Furness, the great American editor who initiated the still incomplete variorum edition of Shakespeare, looked with horror on the future of *Hamlet* criticism, somewhat in the manner of Milton's sour prediction that "so shall the world go on, / Under her own weight groaning" (*Paradise Lost* 12.537, 539), when addressing the Phi Beta Kappa chapter at Harvard University in 1908:[1]

> Lastly, let me entreat, and beseech, and adjure, and implore you not to write an essay on Hamlet. In the catalogue of a library which is very dear to me, there are about four hundred titles of separate editions, essays, commentaries, lectures, and criticisms on this sole tragedy, and I know that this is only the vanguard of the coming years. To modify the words, on another subject, of my ever dear and revered Master, the late Professor Child, I am convinced that were I told that my closest friend was lying at the point of death, and that his life could be saved by permitting him to divulge his theory of Hamlet, I would instantly say, "Let him die! let him die! let him die!"

Perhaps this attitude toward *Hamlet* criticism — enough already — has now become widespread. Why has my generation of literary intellectuals contributed so little to the elucidation of *Hamlet?* There seem to be, generally speaking, two possible explanations. One is that many of us have broken contact with the culture of Romanticism, and expressed outright hatred for the ideal of Romantic individualism that promoted this play to its lofty status in world literature. The other is that we really have had enough already. Let it go! The problems and mysteries of the play have been worked over for three centuries by observant critics and diligent editors. At this late date there is not much fresh and original to be said about *Hamlet;* its critics, from this point of view, are hereafter doomed to be superfluous. If these explanations are correct, then my book might be considered the minority report of a minority ambition. I feel deeply connected to the culture of romanticism, and the history of *Hamlet* criticism intrigues me a lot more than it bores or oppresses me. Let it go on!

As I turned from the history of criticism to the play itself, my work quickly lost its initial polemical edge. Born of a sorrow that my generation of scholar-critics might have embarrassingly little to contribute to the understanding of Shakespeare's major work, the book rapidly became a love affair with *Hamlet.* I did not think of myself as a latecomer relegated to triviality by powerful precursors. Compared to *Oedipus Rex, Hamlet* is still in its infancy. Its tradition is young and open, rich in questions, teeming with opportunity.

And what a start! Shakespeare's revenge tragedy was present at the birth of Romantic individualism, at the early tests of the doctrine of organic unity, at the discovery of the oedipus complex, at the center of the mythy shenanigans in

Joyce's *Ulysses.* It has fascinated Goethe, the Schlegel brothers, Coleridge, Freud, Bradley, Wilson Knight, Dover Wilson, Maynard Mack, Harold Bloom, and Gordon Braden, among others. Works like *Hamlet,* which have been shown over centuries to have enough coherence and mystery to touch off major transformations in Western culture, are both challenges and standing invitations. It is not for me to say whether I have met the challenge, but I accepted the invitation gratefully. The poignance and excitement of writing on a Shakespeare or a Milton is that you probably pass this way just once, and now get your say, your place in the tradition, however ephemeral that may be. My own chance at *Hamlet* went forward in a kind of bliss which I attribute in part to the greatness and cultural heft of the work. I felt lucky to have inherited (from the critics as well as from Shakespeare) so much wit, imagination, judgment, and emotional force.

My bliss might be described more precisely as a love affair between *Hamlet* and the kind of literary criticism I have been trained to write. I am aware of four influences. The first two, literary formalism and historical scholarship, were also the first acquired, and remain the providers of my deepest critical impulses. The next to be appreciated, though not acquired, was intellectual history. All of the reading I did in the 1970s and early 1980s, when I toyed with the new generalities of literary theory, now seems of value to me only inasmuch as it broadened my range as an intellectual historian. I first learned these methods from my undergraduate teachers at Stanford, and their lessons were confirmed in graduate training at Columbia under Edward Tayler, who gave them a beloved personal form. If my abilities in these literary disciplines have improved over the years, some of the credit must also go to Gordon Braden. Signs of our friendship are plentiful in this book. Specifically, I have often taken inspiration from the concluding remarks on *Hamlet* in his magisterial *Renaissance Tragedy and the Senecan Tradition: Anger's Privilege.*

The last influence is psychoanalysis. I have written psychoanalytic literary criticism for twenty years; no doubt this body of theory suffuses the questions I pose and the answers I am predisposed to find satisfactory. Moreover, the Freud-Jones *Hamlet* is still, and deservedly so, the best-known and most-respected psychoanalytic interpretation of a work of art. But psychoanalysis is a more muted presence here than in some of my previous work. I have reached that time in life when one begins throwing away the ladders. The psychoanalytic side of this book is about splitting, and its author, a psychoanalytic reader and a historical reader, is himself a split person with the ambition of achieving fusion.

My second chapter follows the journey of a single phrase, "good night," through the text of *Hamlet.* It is meant as a general introduction to the nocturnal terrors and dilemmas of the play. Imitation is my form of compliment: those familiar with the criticism of Edward Tayler will recognize in the methods and rhetoric of this chapter an admiring student's tribute to its excellence. "Good night" presupposes two divisions, those of day from night and good from evil. The third and fourth chapters, dilating the theme of division, concentrate on Hamlet's split apprehension of women and his attempt to salvage purity from an initial conviction of general debasement. My last chapter treats the self-revised Hamlet of Act 5. Shakespeare begins yoking Christianity and personal vengeance in the graveyard scene, where Hamlet performs before our very eyes an act of identification. A scene later, this remarkable alliance surfaces again in the patient demeanor of the prince, defying augury as he awaits the completion of a revenge both classical and providential. The reader who at any point in these chapters thinks of Thomas Browne will be close to the secrets of the author's design.

My title alludes to Hamlet's attempt to perfect himself, fashioning ideals from an inheritance of disillusionment, and to the perfection of Shakespeare's art. Again and again in the *Hamlet* literature one finds critics who tackle the play with great imaginative excitement, confident in its power to mean and its generous capacity to yield up stores of design and implication to the most rigorous forms of investigation, but who pull back toward the end to note that of course this tragedy is flawed and is by no means Shakespeare's greatest work. The very best critics, A. C. Bradley himself, repeat this gesture. It will not be found here. In *Hamlet* Shakespeare was at the top of his game. The creation of literary criticism able to display his perfected art is throughout my highest aspiration.

Acknowledgments

Edward Tayler, Gordon Braden, Marina Favila, Richard Noland, and Philip White read and improved my manuscript. If mistakes remain, and they usually do, they are of course my responsibility. I also benefited from discussions with Robert Fallon and Murray Schwartz. Philip White constructed the index. Anne Whitmore, my editor at Johns Hopkins University Press, gave me sensible advice on stylistic matters and did her best to slay the hobgoblin of inconsistency. With the support of several Directors of Graduate Studies, I have been teaching Shakespeare to students at the University of Massachusetts for the last five years; my thinking about Shakespeare in general and *Hamlet* in particular took shape in response to theirs. I talked over almost everything in this book with my wife, Dr. Amelia Burnham Kerrigan, and it is not the least of my ambitions to hope that the example of her sharp wits and pungent words made an impression on my prose.

The book is dedicated to my children. May they live as Shakespeare teaches us to live, greatly and fearlessly.

HAMLET'S PERFECTION

1 *Hamlet* in History

A BRIEF POLEMICAL GUIDE FROM
THE ROMANTICS TO THE THEORISTS

It all begins with the Romantic Germans. They determined that *Hamlet* would be what it is today, the main contribution of the English language to world literature. Horace Howard Furness dedicated his monumental New Variorum edition of 1877 to the German Shakespeare Society of Weimar. Is this puzzle-ridden revenge tragedy really Shakespeare's greatest work? Because of the tradition initiated in Germany, the question has become pointless, the world having already decided.

Hamlet has unquestionably been a boon to the theater, generating many versions and attracting the most ambitious producers, directors, and actors in many countries for nearly four centuries. It is by no means clear, however, that the play has been a godsend for literary criticism. This discipline is sometimes rebuked because its procedures are not scientific: only in the rare instance does criticism define a

problem, assess solutions, and arrive at a broad and enduring consensus. At first glance, the history of the criticism on
Hamlet, the very summit of the literary canon, seems a woe-
ful example of this chaotic impressionism. New problems
proliferate; old problems do not go away. When a critic consents to the views of a previous critic, he usually adds qual-
ifications, often idiosyncratic ones.

But things are not as bad as they might appear to the scientific rationalist. The history of *Hamlet* criticism reveals a
finite number of "frameworks" within which specific interpretations unwind. A Heideggerian might call them fore-
conceptions; a breezy pragmatist might prefer to call them
moves.

There are, for example, many moralizing attacks on the
character of Hamlet, charging him with cynicism, cruelty
to Ophelia, unnecessary murder in the case of Rosencrantz
and Guildenstern, and finally, with loyalty to the unchris-
tian ethic of revenge. A large set of counterarguments trace
the purportedly uneasy coexistence of Christianity and the
revenge ethic to the intractable materials in an older play,
the so-called *Ur-Hamlet*, that Shakespeare is believed to
have adapted. Others claim on historical grounds that Christianity never did expunge the revenge ethic: despite centuries of theological condemnation, honor remained a prominent motive in Renaissance culture. These traditions have a
way of improving each other. The moralists make the apol-
ogists more agile, and vice versa. Longstanding differences
generate intellectual energy.

New evaluative history needs to be written, however, because the tradition is today in danger of being discarded
and forgotten. Both words are necessary to my meaning
here, since those who have been trained in a tradition may

discard it, but those who come after, students of the discard-
ers, will be simply oblivious.

Teaching a Shakespeare seminar in 1991, I decided to
prepare for the *Hamlet* class by reading most of the prominently placed criticism of the 1980s. It was during this de-
cade that English departments came under the spell of "literary theory," an umbrella term for criticism featuring the
ideas of Jacques Derrida, Jacques Lacan, Michel Foucault,
and the numerous purveyors of their thinking in England
and America. Renaissance studies produced its own home-
grown theory in the so-called "new historicism," which pur-
ported to break down the ill-conceived boundaries between
literary and nonliterary works in order to recover the ideological forces in Renaissance writing. I knew that theory-
driven criticism tended to be self-canonizing, wanting above
all to have made a difference, and therefore likely to avoid
the debates and uncertainties that had preoccupied earlier
generations of literary intellectuals, but I was not prepared
for the shocking decadence of *Hamlet* criticism from the
1980s. In practice, if this work was any guide, literary theory
seemed to be a blank check for shallow arrogance.

I encountered a criticism that rejected the old motives of
displaying a work of art's emotional and intellectual force
and made no effort to achieve a coherent understanding of
the entire play. One critic, who was fairly interesting until
devastated by literary theory's new looseness of argument,
maintains that the murder of King Hamlet did not occur as
reported by his ghost; Dover Wilson could not tolerate this
truth (for which there is no evidence whatsoever) because,
as he began work on his classic *What Happens in Hamlet*,
he was denying the compelling rectitude of the Bolshevik
Revolution. Another discussion would touch down briefly

on Shakespeare's text, then bounce off into sentences such as "Derrida's allusion to Mallarmé is pertinent, for Mallarmé was a great admirer of Shakespeare's *Hamlet*": strained associations, it would appear, have now become "pertinent." Another writer describes, in unrelieved psychobabble, how Hamlet the dove goes down to Claudius the hawk because he cannot construct a coherent self in a world of double binds. Still another, unconsciously parodying new historicism, supposes the gravedigger to be a "digger" in the sense that word would have during the Puritan Revolution—"a member of a Christian communist sect believing that all lands should be equally distributed among living humans." There is no evidence that the group existed in 1601 or that the word *digger* had any political meaning whatsoever at the turn of the century. Undaunted, the critic proceeds with her fantastic political morality play, finding the climax of the tragedy in Hamlet's contemptuous response to the digger's attempt to sing a courtly song: he who has been appropriating the language of the lower orders cannot bear it when the lowly appropriate the high.[1]

Perhaps *Hamlet* is now a play object for contemporary critics. Their new methods and concerns give them no way to solve its mysteries and unravel its cruxes, so they paw at it, makes gestures at it, and mount mischievous little runs on its margins to catch at least a bit of the crumbling old classic in their nets of intertextuality. But this, to my mind, is cowardice, and a cowardice that leaves the world less interesting. In literary studies there is no substitute—certainly not in self-fulfilling projects such as "deconstruct all oppositions" or "demonstrate that what the Renaissance believed to be nature is in fact culture" or "show that logic is in fact a species of rhetoric"—for the abiding mysteries that we inherit from our predecessors. The state in which they are passed on takes the measure of every generation of critics.

Gary Taylor maintains in a recent book that the bard was in fact a second-rate writer of an unfortunately right-wing bent whose works have been subject to a great deal of ideological distortion, used to proscribe learning, literacy, patriotism, and true cultivation—a club to beat back unwanted novelties of all kinds.[2] Should this view gain prominence, we might see the first generation of critics in two hundred years to refuse the challenge of Shakespeare's greatness. Greatness, no doubt, is a burden; it makes us feel smaller. But it also asks us to rise to the occasion.

Mine is of course a selective history. I have not studied the effect on criticism of theatrical performance, which in this case is probably considerable. I pass over in silence, for reasons already stated in my opening paragraph, the comments of the seventeenth and eighteenth centuries. I leap from the Romantics to A. C. Bradley, and from Bradley to the especially rich criticism of the 1930s. I have sometimes relied on Paul Conklin's *A History of* Hamlet *Criticism, 1601–1821* and on the summaries provided by A. A. Raven in his invaluable *Hamlet Bibliography and Reference Guide, 1877–1935.*[3]

It all begins, as I say, with the Romantic Germans. Critics have perhaps dwelled too long and too often on the remarks of Goethe's Wilhelm Meister, though his image of a gentle, contemplative Hamlet unfitted to the tasks laid on him by the ghost does indeed father a major line in future criticism by stressing Hamlet's resistance to the role of revenger.[4] For Goethe the central lines of the play are, "The time is out of joint. O cursed spite / That ever I was born to set it right."[5] Within the full context of *Wilhelm Meister's Apprenticeship*, Goethe suggests a more ample version of this perception. *Hamlet* is a failed *Bildungsroman* in which the thirtyish hero cannot achieve maturity. For Hamlet there will be no Wittenberg degree, no marriage, no throne, no freedom from the sway of his parents. Circumstances reduce his life to revenge. After the visit of the ghost, he himself performs the reduction, promising to wipe everything from the book and volume of his brain save the injunctions of the ghost. But his resistance to this simplification makes the character. Fortinbras's eulogy is not for the revenger but for the mature future he never enjoyed: "For he was likely, had he been put on, / To have prov'd most royal" (5.2.402–3). In the history of *Hamlet* criticism, interpreters are always repeating unrecognized predecessors. Barbara Everett has recently retrieved the failed *Bildungsroman*.[6]

August Wilhelm Schlegel puts at the center of the play the native hue of resolution sicklied o'er with the pale cast of thought: there, precisely, is the tragedy, "a tragedy of thought."[7] Hamlet never spoke truer than when he noted the distance between himself and Hercules. He falls prey to skepticism: "He has even gone so far as to say 'there is nothing either good or bad, but thinking makes it so'; with him the poet loses himself here in a labyrinth of thought, in which neither end nor beginning is discoverable" (p. 406).

British commentators are generally harsh with these Romantic Germans, and turn with relief to Coleridge, who steals their ideas for the native tradition; but A. W. Schlegel is right about the corrosiveness of skepticism in Shakespeare, as was noted, in effect, by Susanne Türck in her pioneering study of Shakespeare and Montaigne.[8] Whereas the skeptical Montaigne is the calmest of souls, moving with negligent ease through the storehouses of his mind, Hamlet (until Act 5, when he is no longer a skeptic) seems almost constantly agitated; his perception of wayward subjectivity arises in large part from the world's sudden indifference to his dead father, who suffers "not thinking on, with the hobby-horse, whose epitaph is 'For O, for O, the hobby-horse is forgot'" (3.2.132–33). The agony and disillusionment that attend doubt in Shakespeare are also downplayed by A. P. Rossiter and his disciple Graham Bradshaw, who speak of skepticism as if it were a robust contempt for conventional pieties that gave the poet, in dramatic terms, the idea of perpetually undermining himself with healthy irony.[9]

Friedrich Schlegel, close in spirit to his brother, thought Hamlet the first and greatest of the *psychologische Romane*.[10] Shakespeare broke with Aristotelian tragedy by giving character priority over action — a notion that Hegel adopts, and as we will see, passes on to A. C. Bradley. The prince's energies are confined to his mind, where he thinks over his active self, or worldliness in general, losing the name of action. This is close to the view of Coleridge but insists on a historical dimension that drops out, at least with regard to *Hamlet*, in the English critic. As Hamlet delays, as character withholds action, Shakespeare overturns the fundamental principle of classical tragedy.

This historical claim is, I think, one of the main reasons for *Hamlet*'s sudden elevation during the Romantic period. It is not enough to say that these men saw Hamlet in their own image as a moody, thought-laden intellectual. The central fact of a character shaped about a delay in action permitted *Hamlet* to mark the difference between classical and modern. From at least the sixteenth century, European culture had been looking for a satisfactory account of that difference. Now, with *Hamlet* as their rallying point, the Romantics could take aim at the neoclassicists, who were interested in the modern only to condemn its deviation from the classical. They also cleared a place for a modern Aristotle, able to codify the aesthetics of a drama based on pure individualism of character. All of the great Romantic critics, from the Schlegels to G. Wilson Knight, have been trying to discover the new forms that unity, structure, character, action, and style assume in Shakespeare's postclassical drama.

Lets imagine for a moment that the Schlegel brothers are correct, that *Hamlet* is a tragedy of thought and therefore a triumph of character. Does the play, viewed from this perspective, assume a shape that looks plausibly Shakespearean? I think it does, which is not to say that other views are wrong. This is one of the major paradigms in *Hamlet* interpretation, and rather than dismiss it as an artefact of Romantic projection, I want to establish its initial credibility.

This *Hamlet* of course insists on the hero's delay, which there is plenty in the text to support, including the self-reproaches of Hamlet himself. Soliloquies are unusually prominent in the play. The prince has seven of them. Loosely speaking, all soliloquies share a thought-world with the audience, but in this play Shakespeare provides them with a precise rationale. "But break, my heart, for I must hold my tongue," the first one ends, establishing soliloquy as the form in which a candor impossible in public will be indulged. In the seven soliloquies, we hear the Hamlet who knows not "seems," the man who might "put on" an antic disposition.

The prominence of suicide in these privileged communications also makes sense from this angle, for Hamlet wants to kill his tainted flesh, resolving it to dew, but also to destroy his intolerable thoughts: "Must I remember? . . . Let me not think on't" (1.2.143–6). In "To be or not to be," if the usual interpretation is correct, he decides against suicide because of "the dread of something after death"— which is to say, the dread of thoughts after death, a continuation of the bad dreams that poison the "infinite space" of thinking's kingdom. The Mousetrap play catches the conscience of the king, prompting him to divulge thoughts that know not "seems," the very realm in which soliloquy unfolds: in the prayer scene Claudius is in fact given a soliloquy to reveal the thoughts of "occulted guilt" (2.3.80) that Hamlet has trapped for public view. Hamlet does not kill Claudius on this occasion because he himself has not been able to penetrate the "occulted guilt," thinking instead that he will send the repentant king heavenward. Yet Hamlet may have this lost opportunity in mind when he later chides himself for "thinking too precisely on th'event— / A thought which, quarter'd, hath but one part wisdom / And ever three parts coward" (4.4.41–43). Hamlet is often thinking about his thinking: "O, from this time forth / My thoughts be bloody or be nothing worth" (4.4.65–66). A gentleman tells us that Ophelia in her madness "would make one think there might be thought / Though nothing sure, yet much unhappily" (4.5.12–13). In the last act Hamlet praises a new sort of thinking: rashness, the opposite of "thinking too precisely on the event."

Shakespeare often highlights his meaning with dramatic irony. When Hamlet first commits himself to revenge, he asks the ghost to let him know (to become able to think) the circumstances of his murder: "Haste me to know't, that I with wings as swift / As meditation or the thoughts of love / May sweep to my revenge" (1.5.29–31). Shakespeare's works are filled with opposites. The counterpart of the Romantic Hamlet would be Macbeth, who hesitates briefly and then, declaring that "Words to the heat of deeds too cold breath gives" (2.2.61), enacts his bloody thoughts over and over to the point of habit. I could go on, as many critics have, but I hope this interlude has given some solidity to the Romantic *Hamlet*.[11]

Coleridge was incensed that Wordsworth accused him of popularizing the Schlegel *Hamlet*, and left among his papers an oddly legalistic document in which he swears that his interpretation was in his mind before he read A. W. Schlegel's *Lectures*. The twentieth-century editor of his Shakespeare criticism, who makes the best possible case for his author, must nonetheless include footnotes with statements such as "Coleridge has, as usual, somewhat bettered the style of his original [A. W. Schlegel], but the plagiarism is evident."[12] I do not wish to denigrate Coleridge's great influence on Shakespeare studies. Considering the vast library of books and essays that seek to define the unity of *Hamlet* or parts of *Hamlet*, Arthur Eastman must be right to conclude that "the felt concept of organic unity remains still the most fruitful of all the critical awarenesses brought to Shakespeare."[13] On the subject of *Hamlet*, however, Coleridge adds little to the Germans.

Hamlet is again the prince of thought:

In Hamlet I conceive him [Shakespeare] to have wished to exemplify the moral necessity of a due balance between our attention to outward objects and our mediation on inward thoughts—a due balance between the real and the imaginary world. In Hamlet this balance does not exist—his thoughts, images, and fancy [being] far more vivid than his perceptions instantly passing thro' the medium of his contemplations, and acquiring as they pass a form and color not naturally their own. Hence great, enormous, intellectual activity, and a consequent proportionate aversion to real action, with all its symptoms and accompanying qualities. (Raysor, 1:37)

When British and American Shakespeareans dismiss the Schlegel *Hamlet*, a distaste for its philosophical emphasis often figures in the judgment, but Coleridge is in truth more philosophical than his German contemporaries, and the worse for it. While the Germans speak simply of "thought," leaving idealism in the background, Coleridge elaborates a model of the mind that separates "inward thoughts" from "perceptions." One might actually be excited by the first and inattentive to the second. When T. S. Eliot writes of the "dissociation of sensibility," he must be opposing just this separation. Eliot locates the moment of dissociation in the middle of the seventeenth century, with the coming of Cartesianism to England. Coleridge, though, has transformed Hamlet, a creature of 1601, into a supreme sufferer. There could be no such distinction in the Renaissance model of the mind, where thought, however abstract, is no less than the fate of sensory impressions.[14]

Elsewhere Coleridge declares that the prince craves the "indefinite" of thought as opposed to the "definiteness" of perception (Raysor, 2:273). What passages in the play could Coleridge have in mind? Hamlet does have a habit of generalizing, as A. W. Schlegel noticed, but many Shakespearean characters give voice to maxims, proverbs, general principles. His is a sententious theater. There is perhaps something peculiar about Hamlet's perceptions in the graveyard scene. As he picks his way through the skulls he might be said to transform obvious truths into questions requiring Horatio's confirmation: "This might be the pate of a politician which this ass now o'er-offices, one that would circumvent God, might it not?" (5.1.76–79). But it seems odd to say that Hamlet, in proceeding along this rhetorical path, prefers the indefiniteness of thought-created questions to the perceptual exactitude of the skull in hand. His mind appears to be working normally: "There is a skull, but I don't know whose skull, and can therefore enumerate the most satisfying possibilities." Hamlet enters into thought, a world of "might."

What is peculiar, I think, is that he seems to be learning the most elementary truth about death (it comes to all, no matter how great) for the first time. Though we can hear Coleridge behind him, A. C. Bradley tones down the philosophy in Coleridge's philosophical psychology and salvages the point: "That fixed habitual look which the world wears for most men did not exist for him. He was for ever unmaking his world and rebuilding it in thought, dissolving what to others were solid facts, and discovering what to others were old truths. There were no old truths for Hamlet."[15] This is one of those passages where Bradley is indulging in what came to be seen as a bad habit, pretending that Hamlet was a real person with a life outside his play. But that hardly matters, so long as the Hamlet conveyed is an accurate representation of the Hamlet on stage. Here, I think, Bradley has it right. There are no old truths for Hamlet— not the "common theme" of the "death of fathers" ("Why seems it so particular with thee?"), the lust of mothers, our conception through sexual congress, our universal mortality. The playwright had perhaps been reading Montaigne.

Before turning to Bradley, I should note that one great inheritor of the German tradition was Sigmund Freud. I do not intend to survey the history of psychoanalytic *Hamlet* criticism; that has been done, and in considerable detail, by Norman Holland.[16] I do want to pause over the historical elegance of Freud's contribution.

A solution to the problem of Hamlet's delay is first mentioned by Freud in a letter of 1897 to Wilhelm Fliess. Even if Freud had written nothing about Shakespeare in it, we would have occasion to remember this letter, for it is also the first time in his papers that Freud refers to the oedipus complex:

> The idea has passed through my head that the same thing may lie at the root of *Hamlet*. I am not thinking of Shakespeare's conscious intentions, but supposing rather that he was impelled to write it by a real event because his own unconscious understood that of his hero. How can one explain the hysteric Hamlet's phrase "So conscience doth make cowards of us all," and his hesitation to avenge his father by killing his uncle, when he himself so casually sends his courtiers to their death and despatches Laertes [*sic*] so quickly? How better than by the torment roused in him by the obscure memory that he himself had meditated the same deed against his father because of passion for his mother—"use every man after his desert, and who should 'scape whipping?" His conscience is his unconscious feeling of guilt. And are not his sexual coldness when talking to Ophelia, his rejection of the instinct to beget children, and finally his transference of the deed

from his father [*sic*] to Ophelia [*sic*], typically hysterical? And does he not finally succeed, in just the same remarkable way as my hysterics do, in bringing down his punishment on himself and suffering the same fate as his father, being poisoned by the same rival?[17]

When these ideas see print in *The Interpretation of Dreams*, Freud will follow the Schlegels in contrasting *Oedipus Rex*, Aristotle's model tragedy, with the distortions and disguises of *Hamlet*, the great modern tragedy.[18] Hamlet delays his revenge, replacing action with a thought-world of character. Freud simultaneously understands the oedipus complex and Hamlet's delay: a new science has been erected in the inward realm of the first modern character. The tragedy of thought now becomes the tragedy of unconscious thought, which derives its name from *Oedipus Rex*. In Freud's refiguration of the Romantic *Hamlet*, the classic is the unthinkable destiny in the soul of the modern.

In part through the work of Ernest Jones, who published in 1910 a first version of what would achieve its final form nearly forty years later in *Hamlet and Oedipus*, Freud's view of *Hamlet* influences most of the criticism of our century.[19] It is firmly entrenched in popular culture. Olivier's camera, panning from the dead body of the prince to a mirror in which we behold the royal bed of Denmark spread with incestuous sheets, has Freud in mind, and so does Zeffirelli when Mel Gibson and Glenn Close tumble about on her couch of luxury. Pieces of Freud's interpretation are often welcomed by literary critics, particularly in discussions of Hamlet's anger at Gertrude and Ophelia. Sometimes it is criticized as an extreme example of the Bradleyan error of vesting imaginative creations with extratextual life.

Sometimes it is said to be unhistorical, anachronistically imposing a modern theory on a Renaissance work. In this respect, Freud inspired the literary historians who sought to bury him. By showing what an interpretation of *Hamlet* would look like if it were indeed taken as the first great statement of modern character, he encouraged the movement toward a firmer historical grasp of Elizabethan culture, which is no doubt the greatest contribution of the twentieth century to Shakespeare studies in general.

Often Freud's influence is only implicit. I suspect that T. S. Eliot, when he terms *Hamlet* an artistic failure because the hero's anger at his mother is in excess of the facts, lacking an objective correlative, really means to demote the Freudian *Hamlet*, which presupposes exactly this disproportion.[20] Eliot is willing to believe that there might be a Shakespeare play requiring psychoanalysis for its elucidation but must deny that play its customary spot at the apex of English literature.

Trained as a philosopher under T. H. Green, Andrew Cecil Bradley inherited the Romantic *Hamlet* from Coleridge and Hegel. He explains in his *Oxford Lectures* that ancient tragedy was based on moral conflict, whereas modern tragedy is personal, concentrating our interest on "individuality as such": "What engrosses our attention is the whole personality of Hamlet in his conflict, not with an opposing spiritual power, but with circumstances and, still more, with difficulties in his own nature."[21] One of the two lectures devoted to *Hamlet* in *Shakespearean Tragedy* ends with a passage on the Romantic elevation of *Hamlet*. "And this is the reason why, in the great ideal movement which began towards the close of the eighteenth century, this tragedy acquired a position unique among Shakespeare's dramas, and shared only by Goethe's *Faust*. It was not that *Hamlet* is Shakespeare's greatest tragedy or most perfect work of art; it was that *Hamlet* most brings home to us at once the sense of the soul's infinity, and the sense of doom which not only circumscribes that infinity but appears to be its offspring."[22] Bradley sees with full historical clarity what happened in the history of *Hamlet*'s reception, but it is obvious from "brings home to us" that for him the history of Romanticism still unfolds in a living culture.

Bradley's *Hamlet* lectures remain the classic interpretation of the play with delay at its center. He supplants his Romantic precursors by bending the "Schlegel-Coleridge type of theory" (pp. 107–8) into a better fit with the entirety of the text. He serves organic form far better than the Romantics who invented it, and he, more than Coleridge in my view, is the true father of the idea that each Shakespeare play has a distinct "atmosphere" or "world." The Romantics were ever eager to enjoy the sublime, and tended to dwell on great speeches, letting the rest of the drama slip away into incidental felicities or insignificant details. Bradley also seeks sublimity, but he balances these flights with attention to plot construction, style, minor characters, the play as a whole.

The Romantics were wrong to assume that Hamlet's nature was responsible for his tragedy. Hamlet might have kept his bearings save for the melancholy that had poisoned his mind before the visitation of the ghost: the first soliloquy becomes the key to the mystery of Hamlet's character. Hamlet's recoil from his mother—her sensuality, her shallowness, her lack of loyalty—leads to "bewildered horror, then loathing, then despair of human nature" (p. 101). In the Hamlet of Act 5 Bradley sees "a certain change, though it is not great" (p. 119), not great because there is no "effective resolution to fulfill the appointed duty" (p. 120). The passages in which Hamlet might appear to feel himself in the hands of providence actually express "fatalism," "a sad or indifferent self-abandonment" (p. 120).

Such is the general tenor of the interpretation. Future criticism masses about it. Bradley does not appear to have known very much about Elizabethan melancholy. Scores of critics will fill in the gap. Lily Bess Campbell, finding the moral of Shakespearean tragedy in excessive passion, will observe excessive grief at the heart of *Hamlet*.[23] Jacques Lacan, hoping to outdo Freud, will emphasize the prevalence of mourning in the play.[24] Arthur Kirsch will note that "oedipal echoes cannot be disentangled from Hamlet's grief."[25] Many are Bradley's children.

Still, although the general thrust of the reading guided subsequent critics, Bradley's enduring power arises from local observations. I think most of us wouldn't trade five or six of those passages about infinite spirit generating doomed confinement as its dialectical counterpart for his brilliant comment on Hamlet's last words to Claudius. "Here, thou incestuous, murderous, damn'd Dane," Hamlet says, placing in the adjectives a journey from crime to punishment, Claudius's triumph to his triumph, "Drink off this potion. Is thy union here? / Follow my mother." Bradley remarks (p. 126): "The 'union' was the pearl which Claudius professed to throw into the cup, and in place of which (as Hamlet supposes) he dropped poison in. But the 'union' is also that incestuous marriage which must not be broken by his remaining alive now that his partner is dead. What rage there is in the words, and what a strange lightning of the mind!" This is worth hundreds of forgettable essays about

Hamlet's wittiness and love of wordplay. Bradley finds the savagery in Hamlet, and leaves us with the memorable image of a Hamlet who represents his moment of vengeance, come at last, as the son forcing his stepfather to obey his marriage vow. This deserves a place in the annals of sardonic rage.

The rhetorical form of Bradley's lecture on the delay is itself an omen of things to come as well as a sign of things already past. The critic engages in a debate with a list of alternative explanations for Hamlet's procrastination. One senses that organic unity is not a placid assumption for Bradley: the play threatens to fly apart into enigmas and competing explanations, all of which must be considered before *Hamlet* can be got at freshly.

He in part resists the fragmentation by limiting himself to the delay, for him, the problem of problems. But there are, of course, other problems. What do we make, what should Hamlet have made, of the ghost? Did Hamlet, does he, love Ophelia? Why does he put on the antic disposition? Does he really go mad? Is Horatio a Dane? If Horatio was at the funeral of King Hamlet, and the play opens about two months after his death, why has Hamlet not seen him until 1.2? What is the "election" that appears necessary to crown a king in Denmark? The problems keep proliferating. The impressive Jenkins edition of 1981 offers 164 "long notes," many of them worrying new mysteries, such as whether it could be significant that *Polonius* means "man from Polonia [Poland]." As early as 1879 J. O. Halliwell-Phillipps had written: "The more I read of the tragedy of Hamlet the less I understand it as a whole, and now despair of meeting with any theories that will reconcile its perplexing inconsistencies."[26] An article published in 1898 lists ten theories of the delay, then adds two more of its own.[27] All of the major *Hamlet* critics struggle to keep the play coherently before them and, with one major exception, try to find a way to write about this work that avoids the potentially deadening *sic et non* of the crux solvers.

After Bradley there arises a school of interpreters insisting on the priority of action, structure, and convention over character. They think of themselves as scholars, hard-headed literary historians contemptuous of Bradley's "psychologizing." Shakespeare dramatized stories and invented characters to fit the action of these stories. Most of the problems, in their view, stem from ignorance of the conventions of revenge tragedy. Moreover, the architects of the psychologized Hamlet do not seem to realize the full implications of the fact that Shakespeare inherited the *Hamlet* story from a previous play. Some of them (Kuno Fischer, Lorenz Morsbach, Levin Schücking) are German. The cantankerous J. M. Robertson is a British example. Perhaps the most belligerent and persistent of the lot, E. E. Stoll, is American.[28]

It is easy to ridicule their work. To claim that most of the problems discerned by *Hamlet* criticism can be traced to the *Ur-Hamlet*, a lost play, is to solve a mystery with a mystery. But the orientation of these critics toward the actual documents of Elizabethan culture was obviously convincing enough to produce literary scholarship as we know it today, a discipline that ranges from historical research to the refinements of complex literary interpretation. If this discipline began in a battle between armchair critics and gruff historical reductionists, it was not long before the critics learned the ways of the scholars, and much to their profit. How wonderful it is when L. C. Knights, pondering "The readiness is all," can adduce from Thomas Elyot the apt quotation: "'Maturum' in Latin may be interpreted ripe or ready, as fruit when it is ripe, it is at the very point to be gathered and eaten. And every other thing, when it is ready, it is at the instant after to be occupied. Therefore that word maturity, is translated to the acts of men, that when they be done with such moderation, that nothing in the doing may be seen superfluous or indigent, we may say, that they may be maturely done."[29] By dividing *maturum* into "ripe or ready," Elyot neatly clarifies the kinship between *Hamlet*'s "The readiness is all" and *King Lear*'s "Ripeness is all." Knights is a hybrid, a scholar-critic, and the training of a large number of these is probably the single greatest achievement of literary education in the twentieth century.

Though he is not much of a scholar, A.J.A. Waldock, writing in 1931, represents many of the attitudes of Bradley's earlier opponents. The master of character analysis mounted a theory that "neglects first to establish the problem which it seeks to solve."[30] For Hamlet does not delay. He refuses to kill Claudius when at prayer for precisely the reasons stated. This commits Waldock to explaining away the ghost's second visit "to whet thy almost blunted purpose" (3.4.111), and he does. Speculation should be limited to the actual text. Wondering, for example, whether Hamlet has hidden scruples about the revenge ethic "is like asking for news from the fourth dimension" (p. 80). Interpreters should also bear in mind the criterion of what might plausibly be conveyed in the theater. Not for the last time, Bradley's *Hamlet* is declared to be unactable.

The first great book on Shakespeare published in the 1930s, G. Wilson Knight's *The Wheel of Fire*, pierces clean through the contemporary debate between character and action to an engagement with Shakespeare so intense and idiosyncratic that it has neither precedents nor progeny. He apprehends in Shakespeare one vast poem being written in a self-invented aesthetic, riven by searing conflicts between life and death, love and hate, idealism and nihilism, superiority and ordinariness. No one has ever had Shakespeare more fully in mind. Knight seems to have the entire Shakespearean corpus available to him at every moment with equal vividness, the absolute master of unexpected yet illuminating comparison. His values might be described, however improbably, as those of a Nietzschean Christian, and he is not in the least embarrassed to find them in Shakespeare. Hamlet says of his father that "he was a man, take him for all in all," and Knight takes "man" to mean "superman," "an earnest, a symptom, of what humankind should be."[31] It makes a kind of sense. Hamlet's father *is* a god to him, or epitome of the gods, "A combination and a form indeed / Where every god did seem to set his seal / To give the world assurance of a man" (3.4.62). The word *man* in such a passage *does* mean something close to "superman"— man as he might be, magisterial in his endowments. Whereas the psychoanalytic tradition tends always to see oppression in this divinized father, Knight explores the ways in which a human deity might inspire.

Knight's interpretation also offers a choice example of the attacks on the character of Hamlet that appear now and then in a largely sympathetic criticism. Dwelling on "the thought of foulness as the basis of life" (p. 22), Hamlet is the ambassador of death, and he beholds an almost Gnostic world of pestilent vapors, much like the one evoked in the opening speech of Milton's *Comus*. "There is a continual process of self-murder at work in Hamlet's mind" (p. 26), issuing in stunted idealism, callous cruelty, and habitual cynicism. "But the intuitive faith, or love, or purpose, by which we live if we are to remain sane, of these things, which are drawn from a timeless reality within the soul, Hamlet is unmercifully bereft" (p. 28). The critic is not just saying that Hamlet lacks everything that makes life sweet. The power here lies in the word "unmercifully": something awesome and horrible in Shakespeare is beginning to surface in *Hamlet*, a strain of life-denial that will lead eventually to the merciless ranting of Timon. Knight deepens the savagery of Hamlet's ironic "Follow my mother." It is as if he had heard Claudius confess his need for Gertrude, his inability to give up "my queen" (3.3.55) even to save his soul. Hamlet makes death of that love.

"Nothing, I believe," Bradley himself had remarked, "is to be found elsewhere in Shakespeare (unless in the rage of the disillusioned idealist Timon) of quite the same kind as Hamlet's disgust at this uncle's drunkenness, his loathing of his mother's sensuality, his astonishment and horror at her shallowness, his contempt for everything pretentious or false, his indifference to everything merely external" (p. 96). Knight's reading expands on this passage. Putting aside the murder being covered up, Claudius seems a capable king, Gertrude a noble queen, Ophelia a treasure of sweetness, Polonius a tedious but not evil counsellor, Laertes a generic young man.[32] Hamlet pulls them all into death. The ghost becomes devilish in this critic's view.[33] Knight chafes at being put before a play wherein the "demon" of cynicism "has always this characteristic: it is right" (p. 39).

Of course, as later critics remark, the murder of Hamlet's father seems rather a lot to ignore in judging the health of the Danish court. Knight himself was dissatisfied with the essay, and in a subsequent edition of *The Wheel of Fire* added a new chapter called "*Hamlet* Reconsidered." Here he works outward from "To be or not to be" and the advice to the players to construct an ideal implicit in the character of Hamlet, a desire to redeem his life by acting finely and nobly. Suicide is the first imperfect solution. Submission to providence is the last. The high point for me comes in Knight's illustrating "in action how like an angel" with a description of a good golf swing.

John Dover Wilson's *What Happens in Hamlet*, when put beside his New Cambridge edition of the play, makes him the most influential of *Hamlet*'s critics next to Bradley.[34] What I thought I knew of *Hamlet* as an undergraduate English major was largely a distillation of his work, and I suspect that the same holds good for many English majors today. Little in Wilson is exactly new. He belongs in the pantheon of *Hamlet* criticism not because he changed the topics of conversation but because he approached the traditional "problems" with unmatched liveliness. Wilson is the perfect blend of critic and scholar, whose *Hamlet* synthesizes Bradley and his no-nonsense opponents. One inevitably thinks of him in association with a Shakespeare character: my choice would be Henry V. In him to a superlative degree are the qualities of a certain familiar breed of English intellectual—crisp common sense, fairness, a love of detail, a flair for dispute. He knows that he is addressing the most enigmatic of plays and never doubts that he was born to straighten it out.

Bradley's Hamlet struggles with circumstances or with forces in his own soul. Wilson's Hamlet is engaged in a tense battle with Claudius, his mighty opposite. Critics in the Bradley tradition tend to make light of the Mousetrap strategy, supposing it to be a rationalization for further delay. In Wilson the play scene comes alive with dramatic tension, as the actors present a dumb show that Hamlet has explicitly told them to avoid and Claudius listens with apparent placidity to speeches that might have been expected to tip his hand. When Claudius finally breaks, Wilson makes us feel as never before Hamlet's exultation — and its precariousness, since the very stratagem that catches the conscience of the king reveals to the king the conscience of Hamlet. He also insists on the thwarted political ambitions of the prince. These ambitions are not mentioned until 5.2.65, because everyone in the court and everyone in the original audiences would have understood Hamlet's position from the beginning; a presumption that Hamlet wants the crown explains why the court takes the Mousetrap, where the regicide is the king's nephew, as a grievous offense to Claudius.

Wilson relates the ambiguous treatment of the ghost to uncertainties in Elizabethan attitudes toward the spirit world.[35] He reminds us that Hamlet's horror and disgust at the incest of a marriage between brother-in-law and sister-in-law was an attitude pervasive in the Elizabethan period.[36] The Hamlet of the character critics had not disappeared altogether, however. The prince oscillates between the excitement of rash action and the depression of its thoughtful aftermath (pp. 213–17). Hamlet's antic disposition, though he eventually makes use of it, was first "prompted by his hysteria" (p. 95), and the brothel language hurled at Ophelia is evidence of something deep and uncontrolled in his anger at his mother (pp. 101–34). The critic's bedrock supposition is that *Hamlet* makes sense: all of the apparent enigmas can be rationalized by intelligent criticism and historical learning.

It is perhaps one of the fallacies of the old historicism to believe that, should historical recovery be perfect, all cruxes would disappear. Cruxes never belong to the nature of the beast. They are printer's errors, mistaken transcriptions, conventions and allusions we no longer understand. Behind them is a core of pure meaning at which interpretation aims. But Shakespeare — in the performance of the Quince company in *A Midsummer Night's Dream*, in the bobbles of the players at Elsinore, in *Hamlet* itself, a story "Of accidental judgments, casual slaughters, / Of deaths put on by cunning and forc'd cause / And, in this upshot, purposes mistook / Fall'n on th'inventors' heads," in which the hero dies promising "O, I could tell you," but does not — suggests that an imp of dyslexia lives in art.

Wilson's book might be compared to Roland Mushat Frye's *The Renaissance Hamlet*, which attempts to be an updated version of *What Happens in Hamlet*.[37] We are to have nothing but the facts, *Hamlet* as it would have been received by its original audience. Moments in the play are surrounded with historical anecdotes, emblems, title pages, paintings, tombs, ghost lore, theology, "resistance theory" (the belief that a tyrant could be deposed and the arguments given in support). Since Claudius conforms to the technical criteria for a tyrant, Hamlet fulfills the sacred duty of tyrannicide.[38] Frye's view has scant justification in the play. There are no asides, no furtive conversations indicating Danish awareness of being tyrannized. This is not the Renaissance way: stage tyranny was always represented in broad strokes. What disturbs Hamlet about the reign of Claudius is not how he rules but that he rules.

As the scholar expounds, the critic atrophies. Hamlet becomes a bundle of Elizabethan clichés. Frye has the merit of always putting us in the way of Renaissance materials. It is useful on "The readiness is all" to have a whole slew of Renaissance divines quoted on the importance of our readiness to die, but it is not useful to me in the same way it is useful to Frye. He thinks the line in *Hamlet* has now been correctly and eternally interpreted, while I find myself thinking that it is going to take all my intellect and imagination to define what is unique and unconventional about Shakespeare's readiness. In showing disgust at an incestuous marriage and the hasty remarriage of a widow, Hamlet may in some degree have been a product of his age, sane and sound; but what of his complete disenchantment with the world, his wish to die, his coarse brutality toward Ophelia? One can quote till doomsday Renaissance moralists suggesting that Hamlet is performing "an act of charity" (p. 162) in smiting his mother into a confession of her sin, except Hamlet does not go to his mother as charity personified; he goes to speak daggers and must purge his soul of the matricidal spirit of Nero. Why does the ghost return to prevent this paragon of charity from killing her with poisoned thoughts? Hamlet, Frye concludes, has "discharged his own moral obligation in her case" (p. 166). This is indeed a tillyardized *Hamlet*, flattened by mountains of impertinent learning.

Nothing in the decades following *What Happens in Hamlet* is worthy of lengthy report. Fredson Bowers published his authoritative *Elizabethan Revenge Tragedy* in 1940 and followed fifteen years later with an influential but probably too schematic essay, "Hamlet as Scourge and Minister." C. S. Lewis championed situation and poetry against the confusions of character analysis. Maynard Mack investigated the "world" of the play, his most interesting result being a new respect for the Hamlet of Act 5. There is more to him than the "fatalism" Bradley discerned. His readiness is new, and so is his freedom from an earlier sense of universal corruption. Peter Alexander surmises that King Hamlet and Prince Hamlet belong to different worlds. The father is a prehistoric warrior-king, the stuff of legend, while the son is a university student, a reader, a lover of theater. L. C. Knights cannot believe that the man who would write *Measure for Measure* and create the figure of Cordelia could possibly have sanctioned revenge. Patrick Crutwell can find in *Hamlet* no scruples whatsoever about the ethics of vengeance.[39]

The last unavoidable book, Harry Levin's *The Question of Hamlet*, is in some ways an expansion of Mack's essay. *Hamlet* opens with a question, and is a play of questions, its very ghost a "questionable shape."[40] From the interrogative mood, Levin passes to the dubious, pointing to the many varieties of doubt. He concludes with the ironic. A brilliant and focused study of the player's Hecuba speech is printed as an appendix, but the book itself, despite flashes of illumination, is wayward and inconsistent. The learning is wide but often superficial: told that Kierkegaard had something apparently rich and fascinating to say about Shakespeare's irony, you look it up and the allusion amounts to nothing. Levin wants to give a moment to everyone's *Hamlet*. There are psychoanalytic episodes; Hamlet is manic with others, depressive when alone (p. 51); he puts on the antic disposition as a "means of expressing pent-up emotions" (p. 113), perhaps a case of the effect being confused with the cause. The prince is a transfigured fool (p. 124), but also, and on the next page, Ficino's saturnine genius. He is a skeptic as well. He is in fact all of us, an existentialist Everyman:

We are Hamlet. His circumstances are ours, to the extent that every man, in some measure, is born to privilege and anxiety, committed where he has never been consulted, hemmed in on all sides by an overbearing situation, and called upon to perform what must seem an ungrateful task. No wonder he undertakes it with many misgivings, tests it with much groping and some backsliding, pursues it with revisions and indecisions, and parses every affirmation by the grammar of doubt. (P. 43)

I hear bongo drums. To think that, after centuries of puzzlement, the sweet prince turns out to be *us*, just another slob on the job, crawling between earth and heaven, struggling with his commitments.

Levin plays many parts, though, and some of them have a future. Here he is descanting on "Lamound" (F) or "Lamord" (Q2), the horseman "incorps'd and demi-natur'd / With the brave beast" (4.7.86–87):

Do we perceive in the centaur-like description, another emblem of man in his animal guise? Or may we take a hint from the Quarto reading, where the Frenchman's name is spelled Lamord? Could that have been, by an easily possible slip of typography or pronunciation, La Mort? And could that equestrian stranger be a premonitory vision of Death on a pale horse, heralding the outcome of the duel? That vision appears unexpectedly in familiar places; in the squares of Paris, as Rilke imagined them, Madame Lamort, the fateful dressmaker, winds and binds the restless ways of the world. (P. 95)

It is more likely that Claudius is praising the oneness of horse and rider for which equestrians have always striven;

G. Wilson Knight was reminded of Prince Hal before the battle, dropped like an angel on a fiery Pegasus to "witch the world with noble horsemanship" (*1H4* 4.1.104–10). In the string of questions, moving into realms of ever thinner possibility, and the final triumphant escape into a tissue of irrelevant associations, this resembles nothing so much as postmodernism, and is in fact cited for its suggestiveness in a recent assay of Lamordian intertextuality.[41] The evolution is clear. Postmodernism is but the most recent state of comp lit *belles-lettres*.

There, according to me, is the tradition of *Hamlet* criticism. I have no doubt missed some major achievements, especially in notes and articles, which I have not had the heart to tackle as thoroughly as the books. But ripeness is all, and I now come to my concluding question. What might the tradition do? Where are its most promising bits of unfinished business?

We might (we of course will) go on arguing about character and action, critics and scholars. When Schlegel proposed that *Hamlet* was the first modern drama, he set a problem that no amount of historical scholarship can resolve. For finally it is a literary call. It hardly matters that much of Renaissance dramatic theory was still wedded to Aristotle: Shakespeare might have been an original. The approach to drama through character is of course fraught with dangers. Characters are subjective—played one way yesterday, played another way tomorrow. The best way to reduce this subjective element is to anchor discussions of character in the details of literary form.

Some postmodernists argue that wordplay in Shakespeare sweeps right through character, replacing the illusion of selfhood with the twists and turns of linguistic

operations. Yet the results of unnumbered formalist interpretations promise that wordplay lends to Shakespearean
characters their specific fortunes and ironies. In *Romeo and
Juliet*, for example, the nurse twice tells the story of how
two-year-old Juliet fell forward, bumped her head, and
cried until the nurse's husband picked her up and in a
bawdy spirit remarked that one day she would fall back-
wards, at which point little Juliet stopped crying and said
"Ay." One is hardly surprised, since this is Shakespeare, that
her first words in the balcony scene are "Ay, me" (2.2.25).
"Dost thou love me? I know thou wilt say 'Ay,'" she
declares some lines further on (90), but she does not want
Romeo to swear a vow, because in that case he might play
false. When she asks the nurse for news after the slaying of
Tybalt, it is with "Ay me, what news?" (3.2.36); in her mistaken assumption that the feared news is Romeo's death,
"ay" becomes a mere sound, a vowel, that can emerge into
significance as three different words, "ay," "I," and "eye":

> Hath Romeo slain himself? Say thou but "Ay"
> And that bare vowel "I" shall poison more
> Than the death-darting eye of cockatrice.
> I am not I if there be such an "I"
> Or those eyes shut that make thee answer "Ay."
> If he be slain say "Ay," or if not, "No."
> Brief sounds determine of my weal or woe.
>
> (3.2.45–51)

Does character here dissolve into a ping-pong of signifiers?
It seems obvious that, to the contrary, wordplay gives to
Juliet — as later to Hamlet, Lear, and Macbeth — the coherence of a destiny. The two-year-old's "Ay" to the thought of
sexual love is the first of many premonitions that shadow

her life. Love itself arrives with a timorous "Ay, me," and the possibility of her "I" and "eye" receiving the news of Romeo's death prefigures the end of her star-crossed story. The very last couplet of the play returns to the rhyme of "no" and "woe": "For never was a story of more woe / Than this of Juliet and Romeo." The lovers say "ay" but fate says "no." Juliet, sensing that truth, greets love with "Ay, me," a yes aware of no; and literary form, the vehicle of fate, rhymes "no" with "woe" and waits until the perfect moment to add, in closing, "Romeo." Brief sounds indeed determine of weal or woe. Shakespeare tells stories about coherent fictive individuals. In what other terms could it possibly make sense to speak of their weal or woe? An awareness of literary devices, and behind them the raw energy of language itself, combining and splitting, is not inconsistent with the apprehension of character.

I would be reluctant to give up the primacy of character in Shakespeare studies, for that seems tantamount to giving up individualism. That loss, in turn, is part and parcel of our current decadence. Stephen Greenblatt famously concludes his *Renaissance Self-Fashioning* with the declaration that he had started to write a book on Renaissance individuals but discovered in the end that there are no individuals.[42] One is somewhat amazed to learn at the beginning of his *Shakespearean Negotiations* that he started this book, too, in a quest for the writer's unique intensity but discovered in the end that there are no writers: "This book argues that works of art, however intensely marked by the creative intelligence and private obsession of individuals, are the products of collective negotiation and exchange."[43] Postmodernism also repudiates unique selfhood. For Terry Eagleton, "Hamlet has no 'essence' of being whatsoever, no inner sanctum to be safeguarded: he is pure deferral and diffusion, a hollow void which offers nothing determinate to be known"—a passage that accurately describes itself and the school it represents.[44] The evidence is in. Give up on individualism and literary acumen deteriorates. We get ideology rather than ideas. We get discussions of culture that glimpse no horizons beyond "containment" and "subversion." We get the bland modern pride known as "political correctness," with its presumption that we might become creatures unable to give offense and people without a cultural center, our shameful xenophobias ground down to a numb universal tolerance.

The scholars in this history have been the ones most suspicious of character. I was trained by scholars, and speaking of "character development" in *Hamlet* makes me uneasy. But I do not know how else to describe the shift from the self-loathing Hamlet of the final two soliloquies to the beautifully calm Hamlet of Act 5. Bradley speaks of "a sad or indifferent self-abandonment." Recently Harold Bloom, probably with this passage in mind, has denied the sadness: "Except for the scheme of Claudius and Laertes, we and the prince might be confronted by a kind of infinite standoff. What seems clear is that the urgency of the earlier Hamlet has gone. Instead, a mysterious and beautiful disinterestedness dominates this truer Hamlet, who compels universal love precisely because he is beyond it, except for the exemplification of Horatio. . . . Not nihilism but authentic disinterestedness, and yet what is that? No Elizabethan lore, no reading in Aristotle, nor even in Montaigne, can help to answer that question. We know the ethos of disinterestedness only because we know Hamlet."[45] Perhaps if we read Seneca? This is well and good, but somewhere in the disinterestedness there is also a shell of furious hatred, jacked and ready. We should study the Hamlet who returns from the sea.

If *Hamlet* were a very good play, a very good modern play, the analysis of his last disposition would lead us inexorably, through many surprising developments, to his first. The "melancholy," as Bradley calls it, is primarily compounded of an anger toward his mother. He grieves, yes. But when Hamlet says "Nay, madame, I know not 'seems'" his grief is in some measure a public demonstration of what *she* should be doing, as Levin Schücking noticed long ago: "His words about his dead father are full of that piteous tenderness which tells of a wound unhealed . . . they breathe the aspiration of a noble heart to offer the deceased in his thoughts a kind of compensation, by means of his passionate admiration, for the wrong done to his memory by the indifference of his widow and the speedy forgetfulness of the others."[46] A main novelty of the Jenkins edition is his suggestion that Hamlet's horror of Gertrude is enough all by itself to motivate his repudiation of Ophelia. Previous editors, most critics, and all the productions I have seen imagine that Hamlet overhears Polonius and Claudius scheming or enters before they are fully concealed—that he has, whatever the stage business, a reason to believe that Ophelia is a conspirator.[47] It seems likely that Hamlet's loathing for Gertrude determines more than we once realized. So we need to understand Hamlet's beginning and his end, and need to put them together. Modern Aristotles puzzling out the mysterious tragedy of character, we must connect beginning, middle, and end.

That's the way it's done.

2 *Hamlet's* Good Night

Polonius must have been thinking of the wearyingly the-
oretical Polonius when he said that to inquire "Why day
is day, night night, and time is time, / Were nothing but to
waste night, time, and day" (2.2.88–89). For works of art
often establish their greatness by illuminating everything
implicit in an ordinary piece of language, such that those
who speak this language feel awakened from their habitual
stupor. *Hamlet* performs this service for "good night,"
from Middle English to modern English our daily formula
for the last departures of the day, sending us from society to
the privacy of bed and sleep.

According to the OED, the full formula was originally
"have good night" or "(God) give you good night," convey-
ing an element of subdued prayer that drops from view in
the shortened form, which most of us today probably take
to mean "I wish you a good night," the complement to

"Have a nice day."[1] Why should the last social act of the day be a ritual formula for making the night good? Because, obviously, night is not good. Every culture mythologizes the difference between day and night.[2] The Renaissance version of this difference has not been lost to us, though I expect that electricity has diminished somewhat the old terrors of the night.

In the mid-seventeenth century Josua Poole culled from many English poets, including Shakespeare and Milton, epithets for commonly personified nouns. The list for "night" includes freezing, dreary, swarthy, gloomy, sullen, dampish, tedious, pitchy, grisly, grim, sullied, collied, hideous, ghastly, palefaced, solitary, melancholy, sober, grave, blind, darksome, secret, thievish, wanton, lascivious, amorous, dumb, hushed, speechless, forgetful, dreadful.[3] Night, one gathers, is long, cold, and solemn. Grave and sober, it is associated with learning; Milton's scholarly "Il Penseroso" begins his day at night. It is a time for thieves and secret plots.[4] It is mournful: the sharpest agonies of mourning are suffered at night.[5] It is sexuality's time. "Though Love and all his pleasures are but toys," Campion conceded, "they shorten winter nights." In this context bidding good night can bless the consummation of a wise marriage; Donne entitled the final section of his Somerset epithalamion "The good-night."[6] But the preponderance of Poole's epithets reveal that the poetry of night lies mostly in its badness.

I turn to Milton—who in his blindness knew "ever-during dark / . . . from the cheerful ways of men / Cut off"—for information on some of the learned items comprising this general badness.[7] He wove some of night's commonplaces into the vast design of *Paradise Lost*. Eve's curiosity about the meaning of starlight is one of the clear routes to the fall, prompting Satan to bring her a dream of nocturnal exaltation. At the court of Chaos the devil had already encountered "Sable-vested *Night*, eldest of things, / The consort of his reign" (2.962–63). Adam's reply to Eve's curiosity alludes to this cosmological detail. Stars shine "Lest total darkness should by Night regain / Her old possession, and extinguish life / In Nature and all things" (4.665–67). The passage alerts us to the fact that terms such as "the dead season," commonly in use for "night" in the English Renaissance, were not felt to be altogether metaphorical.[8]

At Cambridge Milton was assigned a Latin oration on "Whether Day or Night is the More Excellent."[9] In Hesiod, Night (*Nyx*, Roman *Nox*) was the eldest daughter of the primordial Chaos.[10] Embroidering on this material, Milton tells us that the goddess was pursued by Phanes, a rejected suitor. Driven back on her own family, she entered an incestuous marriage with her brother Erebus (Darkness), "a husband who was certainly very like herself" (223). The tale is a "learned and elegant allegory of antiquity" (224) in which Phanes represents the sun. He was not a loving suitor, but a figure of "innate and unremitting hatred," "for it is well known that light and darkness have been divided from one another by an implacable hatred from the very beginning of time" (224–25). Day and night, as Shakespeare put it in Sonnet 28, are "enemies to either's reign;" Viola in *Twelfth Night* promises to keep her love vow "as true in soul / As doth that orbed continent the fire / That severs day from night" (5.1.270–72), which implies that the severance, first enjoined by God in Genesis 1.4, is absolute. From the union of Nyx and Erebus stem the Parcae, Discord, Sleep, Death, Complaint, Fraud, and her last child, Charon. What could be expected, given the character of the mother? The proverb "from a bad crow a bad egg" is exactly applicable to this case (225), a proverbial crow being chosen here, no doubt, because the real crow is both noisome and black.

Switching from Hesiod to Moses, Milton proposes that day is actually older than night, since the primordial chaos prior to creation cannot properly be called night. All creatures instinctively hate night, and hasten to shelter:

> None may be seen abroad save thieves and rogues who fear the light, who, breathing murder and rapine, lie in wait to rob honest folk of their goods, and wander forth by night alone, lest day betray them. . . . None will you meet save ghosts and spectres, and fearsome goblins who follow in Night's train from the realms below; it is their boast that all night long they rule the earth and share it with mankind. . . . Hence clearly is revealed that man's deceit who says that night brings respite from their fears to men and lulls every care to rest. How false and vain is this opinion they know well from their own bitter experience who have ever felt the pangs of guilty conscience; they are beset by Sphinxes and Harpies, Gorgons and Chimaeras, who hunt their victims down with flaming torches in their hands; those poor wretches too know it full well who have no friends to help or succour them, none to assuage their grief with words of comfort, but must pour out their useless complaints to senseless stones, longing and praying for the dawn of day. For this reason did that choicest poet Ovid rightly call Night the mighty foster-mother of cares. (231)

At night ill spirits from the lower world possess the earth. Guilty consciences suffer, as the harpies of revenge find their mark; one thinks of the midnight soliloquy of the suddenly guilty Richard III: "O coward conscience, how dost thou afflict me! / The light burns blue. It is now dead midnight" (5.3.179–80). Night as the realm of ghosts, witches, and crime is rendered almost schematically by Macbeth, the guilty murderer:

Now o'er the one half world
Nature seems dead, and wicked dreams abuse
The curtain'd sleep; witchcraft celebrates
Pale Hecat's off'rings; and wither'd Murther,
Alarum'd by his sentinel, the wolf,
Whose howl's his watch, thus with his stealthy pace,
With Tarquin's ravishing strides, towards his design
Moves like a ghost.[11]

(2.2.49–56)

Evil contains its own judgment. Donne explains to his congregation that night is hell, nature's figure for damnation. "The dayes which God made for man were darknesse, and then light, still the evening and the morning made up the day. The day which the Lord shall bring upon secure and carnall man, is darknesse without light, judgements without any beams of mercy shining through them."[12] Evoking the horror of damnation in one of his best passages, Donne writes out of his age's deep fears of night:

Horrendum est, when Gods hand is bent to strike, *it is a fearefull thing, to fall into the hands of the living God*; but to fall out of the hands of the living God, is a horror beyond our expression, beyond our imagination.

That God should let my soule fall out of his hand, into a bottomless pit, and roll an unremoveable stone upon it, and leave it to that which it finds there, (and it shall finde there, which it never imagined, till it came thither) and never thinke more of that soule, never have more to doe with it. That of that providence of God, that studies the life and preservation of every weed, and worme, and ant, and spider, and toad, and viper, there should never, never any beame flow out upon me; that that God, who looked upon me, when I was nothing, and called me when I was not, as though I had been, out of the womb and depth of darknesse, will not looke upon me now, when, though a miserable, and a banished, and a damned creature, yet I am his creature still, and contribute something to his glory, even in my damnation; that that God, who had often looked upon me in my foulest uncleannesse, and when I had shut out the eye of the day, the Sunne, and the eye of the night, the Taper, and eyes of all the world, with curtaines and windowes and doores, did yet see me. . . . That that God should loose and frustrate all his own purposes and practises upon me, and leave me, and cast me away, as though I cost him nothing, that this God at last, should let this soule goe away, as a smoake, as a vapour, as a bubble, but must lie in darknesse, as long as the Lord of light is light itselfe, and never a sparke of that light reach to my soule. What Tophet is not Paradise . . . to this damnation, to be secluded eternally, eternally, eternally from the sight of God?[13] (5:266–67)

Here we see an entire Christian universe organized about day and night. God is light, his Son a sun, and those who dwell with him dwell in everlasting day. Sinners shut out the light, and eventually are themselves shut out in an endless night of isolation and deprivation. The light invented by men to oppose night, the taper, represents life itself, as we know from Donne's "We' are Tapers too, and at our own cost die" in "The Canonization," Othello's "but once put out thy light / . . . I know not where is that Promethean heat / That can thy light relume" (5.2.10–13), and Macbeth's "Out, out brief candle!"[14] Far from spurning the commonplace, the literary invention of the period welcomed it, trusted it, and through it pursued "thoughts beyond the reaches of our souls" (*Hamlet* 1.4.56). Donne cannot imagine the fearfulness of falling out of the hands of the living God, but in everyday hyperboles of night reaches toward "a horror beyond our expression, beyond our imagination."

I quote in full Fulke Greville's remarkable poem on the innate bond between night and human imagination:

In night when colours all to black are cast,
Distinction lost, or gone down with the light;
The eye a watch to inward senses plac'd,
Not seeing, yet still having power of sight,

Gives vain alarums to the inward sense,
Where fear stirred up with witty tyranny,
Confounds all powers, and thorough self-offence,
Doth forge and raise impossibility:

Such as in thick depriving darknesses,
Proper reflections of the error be,
And images of self-confusednesses,
Which hurt imaginations only see;
    And from this nothing seen, tells news of devils,
    Which but expressions be of inward evils.[15]

The thick depriving darkness of the night reflects the thick depriving darkness of the inward "error," what Donne calls "a darke vapor or *original sinne*" (3:355). In hurt imaginations night breaks down the "distinction," not just between objects, but between inward and outward, leading men to behold in self-confusedness the devils of their own interior hells. Superstition is guilt in action.

An insightful Claudius observes that prayer has "this twofold force, / To be forestalled ere we come to fall / Or pardon'd being down" (3.3.48–50). The piece of ordinary language spoken at the end of the day carried the first of these forces. When someone was bade good night in the English Renaissance, he was wished protection against ghosts and demons, sleeplessness and bad dreams, attacks of guilty conscience and fits of mourning, his criminality and that of others, death and damnation. These fates lie coiled in the nocturnal plot of *Hamlet*.

Hamlet opens at midnight on the battlements of Elsinore with the brief history of a lucky man. Francisco is relieved by the next watch. His has been a quiet watch, "not a mouse stirring" (1.1.11). Horatio and Marcellus arrive. Before they can begin another story, Francisco finishes his, saying good night twice in the full original formula, "Give you good night" (17, 19). He exits posthaste, never to be heard from again. Francisco has no complex function. He simply marks the time and place at which the tragedy begins, then gets out of the way, letting it begin. But his formal good-nights linger over the scene he departs, and to that extent over the entire play.

Certainly the scene dramatizes a night that is not good, the sort of night in view of which "Give you good night" owes its enduring popularity. Horatio's first words to the ghost are "What art thou that usurp'st this time of night" (49). We later learn from the ghost himself that he does, precisely, usurp the time of night, his time on earth coextensive with nighttime: "I am thy father's spirit, / Doom'd for a certain term to walk the night, / And for the day confin'd to fast in fires" (1.5.9–11); Hamlet anticipates this exact correlation when he says that the ghost is "making night hideous" (1.4.54).

If we think of the play as having a nightmind, a largely unconscious one, the ghost is its most conspicuous presence. Hamlet at the beginning of the play already dwells on the fringes of the nightmind. The ghost pulls him in more deeply: "O God, I could be bounded in a nutshell and count myself a king of infinite space—were it not that I have bad dreams" (2.2.254–56). By the end of the play he will be its master. Ophelia sends floral messages as she drifts into the nightmind. The division of day and night in *Hamlet* serves as prologue to a play of primitive divisions. In Chapters 3 and 4 we will see how the hive of Hamlet's brain is riven by splits and failed splits. In Chapter 5 we will explore a striking refiguration of the nightmind.

After the ghost departs at the crowing of the cock, the "trumpet of the morn" who awakes "the god of day," the shaken group on the battlements discuss the divine services of this bird:

> *Marcellus*. It faded on the crowing of the cock.
> Some say that ever 'gainst that season comes
> Wherein our Saviour's birth is celebrated,
> This bird of dawning singeth all night long;
> And then, they say, no spirit dare stir abroad,
> The nights are wholesome, then no planets strike,
> No fairy takes, nor witch hath power to charm,
> So hallow'd and so gracious is that time.

Horatio. So have I heard and do in part believe it.
But look, the morn in russet mantle clad
Walks o'er the dew of yon high eastward hill.

(1.1.162–72)

Horatio's response implies that the cock's night-long songs
in preparation for Christmas are a familiar datum in Danish or British folklore. But no scholar has ever been able to
locate a single reference to this belief, and it seems likely
that Shakespeare invented the whole business. His imaginary folklore perfects the logic of "(God) give you good
night." The cock welcomes "our Saviour's birth," promising the dawn of resurrection by saying good morrow to
Christianity and good night to the evils of the darkness.
Such wholesome "nights" would be protected at every moment by the crowing "goods" of the Lord.

In the next scene, Hamlet comes before us wearing the
"nighted colour" (68), the "inky cloak" and "customary
suits of solemn black" (77–78) that to this day identify him
in the popular imagination. Hamlet wears black, and he is
too much in the sun. I do not want to turn *Hamlet* into a
belated piece of solar mythology descended from prehistoric Germanic invaders, but it seems to me useful at this
point in the play to think of Hamlet as a near personifica-
tion of night.[16] He is mournful, secretive, melancholy, and
about to be haunted. He has "that within which passes
show, / These but the trappings and the suits of woe" (85–
86), which is to say that the true blackness and true inki-
ness are worn within him.

The darkness steals forth in the first soliloquy. Surely the
main burden of the speech is to put before us a mind
damaged by the incestuous marriage of a shallow and sen-

sual mother. It would be straining things to explore these matters in the context of night, and I will postpone some of them until the next chapter, but the association between Hamlet and night so strongly established in the opening scenes is not abandoned entirely in the first soliloquy.

"O that this too too sullied flesh would melt, / Thaw and resolve itself into a dew, / Or that the Everlasting had not fix'd / His canon 'gainst self slaughter" (1.2.129–32). Hamlet yearns to be free of the flesh that is his kinship with his mother. He represents his body as sullied and frozen; perhaps the image is that of smutched snow or ice. The contrast between the unclean and frozen flesh and the dew he wishes it to become implies a movement from cold night ("sullied" fits in neatly with the idea of darkness, and is found among Poole's epithets for night) to dawning day. Dew, a great blessing in the Old Testament (Deut. 33.28 and elsewhere), figures in the manna episode in Exodus 16 and is commonly associated with God's bounty. I take it that the resolution of flesh into dew constitutes an alternative to "self slaughter." Flesh ought not to have touched a mother—and I think a father as well. Hamlet wants to be reborn as a child of heaven, parentless and pure, like the soul of Marvell's "On a Drop of Dew." Because this fantasy cannot be achieved, he contemplates suicide.

Everything in the first soliloquy seems to await the coming of the ghost. Already he is enraged at his mother and contemptuous of his stepfather. Already he is attracted to suicide but trapped in an unwanted life. Already in his prophetic soul remembering is painful ("Must I remember?"). It is the portrait of a mind that will be jolted into fevered extremity by the forthcoming revelations of the ghost. The metaphor of emerging from a frozen night into a dewy dawn connects his wished purification to the withdrawal of the ghost at the crow of the cock. One problem with the notion that Shakespeare critics should limit themselves to interpretations able to be conveyed in the theater is that his works are poems as well as dramas, written in the dedication to inventive coherence that we have learned to expect in the Renaissance lyric: "resolve itself into a dew" punningly foreshadows the ghost's dawn-prompted "Adieu, adieu, adieu. Remember me" (1.5.91). Hamlet at some level resists the ghost.

The revelations of a darkened spirit continue. "O God! God! / How weary, stale, flat, and unprofitable / Seem to me all the uses of this world!" "Uses of this world" here means "customs" or perhaps "morally beneficial maxims to be drawn from this world," as in the Duke's "uses of adversity" in *As You Like It*. But from the Latin *usus*, "uses" carries also a suggestion of ownership, things that can be put into use or exchanged in a marketplace—hence the force of "unprofitable." Hamlet has lost his sympathetic connection to the ordinary daylight world of getting and spending, desiring and affecting. He repeatedly speaks of his poverty: "Give me one poor request" (1.5.148), "so poor a man as Hamlet is" (1.5.192), "Beggar that I am, I am even poor in thanks" (2.2.272). Beholding "an unweeded garden / That grows to seed; things rank and gross in nature / Possess it merely" (1.2.135–37), he finds in the world at large his own suicidal distaste for industry.

What has already been poisoned in young Hamlet? What, I think, Milton conveyed so beautifully in his description of the garden world of *Paradise Lost*:

A wilderness of sweets; for Nature here
Wanton'd as in her prime, and play'd at will
Her Virgin Fancies, pouring forth more sweet,
Wild above Rule or Art, enormous bliss.

(5.294–97)

Sweet is a charged word in Milton's poem, representing what Eden is but would not seem to man without the higher sweetness of a loving marriage. There is no sweetness in Hamlet's garden world: things rank and gross in nature possess it merely, as they possess the world at night. Gertrude attributes his mourning to something "sweet and commendable in your nature" (1.2.87) and later, in the closet scene no less, refers to him as "sweet Hamlet" (3.4.96), but the Hamlet we observe seems a bitter exile from the sessions of sweet silent thought. His gifts and letters, Ophelia remembers, were accompanied by "words of so sweet breath compos'd / As made the things more rich" (3.1.98–99). Marriage to the flower-loving Ophelia, memorably eulogized in Gertrude's "sweets to the sweet" (5.1.236), might have lifted the bitter night from Hamlet's soul, but she falls victim to the global misogyny inspired by his mother.

"It is not, nor it cannot come to good." There is no daylight good to pose against night's disillusionments. In place of benediction we find impotent defiance. "O God! God!" "Fie on't, ah fie." "Heaven and earth! / Must I remember?" The sentiments of the first soliloquy might be described as an inversion of "give you good night"— a "bad morrow" and "bad night" to the hasty and incestuous couple now occupying the throne room at Elsinore, waiting for night to retire to "incestuous sheets." Hamlet loathes the marriage to the depths of his soul.

At first the visitation of the ghost in "the dead waste and middle of the night" (1.2.198) seems to give Hamlet the worldly purpose he lacks in the first soliloquy. He himself represents the effect as no less than the acquisition of a new past:

Yea, from the table of my memory
I'll wipe away all trivial fond records,
That youth and observation copied there,
And thy commandment all alone shall live
Within the book and volume of my brain,
Unmix'd with baser matter.

(1.5.98–104)

Now, surely, he has both a task and a motive. We sense renewal in his attempt to dismiss Horatio and Marcellus: "I hold it fit that we shake hands and part, / You as your business and desire shall point you— / For every man hath business and desire, / Such as it is" (1.5.134–37). Basking in the success of The Mousetrap, Hamlet savors the idea of profitable action in terms dear to Shakespeare himself:

Hamlet. Would not this, sir, and a forest of feathers, if the rest of my fortunes turn Turk with me, with Provincial roses on my razed shoes, get me a fellowship in a cry of players?
Horatio. Half a share.
Hamlet. A whole one, I.

(3.2.269–74)

He has it made—twice as much good fortune as Horatio imagines.

Night becomes in his imagination the figure of a true avenger, the blood-drenched killer he must impersonate in obeying the ghost's "sole commandment." When the players arrive, Hamlet remembers a tragedy about Dido and Aeneas, and in particular "One speech in't I chiefly loved." In order to jar the memory of the actor, he is able to recite twelve and a half lines of this beloved declamation:[17]

> If it live in your memory, begin at this line — let me see, let
>   me see —
> *The rugged Pyrrhus, like th'Hyrcanian beast —*
> 'Tis not so. It begins with Pyrrhus —
> *The rugged Pyrrhus, he whose sable arms,*
> *Black as his purpose, did the night resemble*
> *When he lay couched in the ominous horse,*
> *Hath now this dread and black complexion smear'd*
> *With heraldry more dismal. Head to foot*
> *Now is he total gules, horridly trick'd*
> *With blood of fathers, mothers, daughters, sons,*
> *Bak'd and impasted with the parching streets,*
> *That lend a tyrannous and a damned light*
> *To their lord's murder. Roasted in wrath and fire,*
> *And thus o'ersized with coagulate gore,*
> *With eyes like carbuncles, the hellish Pyrrhus*
> *Old grandsire Priam seeks.*
> So proceed you.[18]
>
>   (2.2.444–61)

The tiger, "th'Hyrcanian beast," is not right, leaving to a future poet the discovery of a tiger burning bright in the forests of the night. The true first line of the chiefly loved speech ends in "he whose sable arms," and out of "sable" emerges the chain of associations down which Hamlet's memory travels: from "sable" to "black" to "night" to "ominous" to "dread and black" to "more dismal," then, night becoming a killer, black yielding to the reds of blood and fire, to "total gules," "horridly," "blood," "bak'd and impasted," "parching," "a tyrannous and a damned light," "roasted in wrath and fire," "coagulate gore," "carbuncles," and finally, the cosmic summary of this dire unfolding, "hellish." The mournful melancholy night of Act 1 has now reemerged as a Senecan avenger armed with death and damnation.

Act 3 is Hamlet's night. Having caught the conscience of the king, he hastens to his midnight appointment with the queen, and as he does so incarnates the murderous Pyrrhus:

> 'Tis now the very witching time of night,
> When churchyards yawn and hell itself breathes out
> Contagion to this world. Now could I drink hot blood,
> And do such bitter business as the day
> Would quake to look on. Soft, now to my mother.
> O heart, lose not thy nature. Let not ever
> The soul of Nero enter this firm bosom;
> Let me be cruel, not unnatural.
> I will speak daggers to her, but use none.
> My tongue and soul in this be hypocrites:
> Now in my words somever she be shent,
> To give them seals never my soul content.[19]

> (3.2.379–90)

In the full tide of Senecan rant, conjuring the iconography of nocturnal terror, Hamlet encounters an impediment. Slowing down and quieting down, he halts his speech with "soft" ("used as an exclamation with imperative force, either to enjoin silence or deprecate haste").[20] He is to visit his mother, not his stepfather; she must be left to heaven. But it is clear that some portion of Hamlet wants the dark avenger to visit his mother, since the rest of the speech is a serious effort at self-command. The avenger must be satisfied with words. "Break, my heart, for I must hold my tongue," the first soliloquy concludes. Now soul is confined to words, unable, like a hypocrite, to put the seals of action on verbal daggers.

The diversion of lurid deeds into lurid words, losing the name of action, is of course characteristic of Hamlet. In the middle acts of the play he cannot escape mutations of his initial melancholy. Once the uses of the world seemed weary, stale, flat, and unprofitable; but after Hamlet is given the task of vengeance, he repeatedly diagnoses these traits in himself. An actor with his own "motive and . . . cue for passion,"

> 　　　would drown the stage with tears,
> And cleave the general ear with horrid speech,
> Make mad the guilty and appall the free,
> Confound the ignorant, and amaze indeed
> The very faculties of eyes and ears.
> Yet I,
> A dull and muddy-mettled rascal, peak
> Like John-a-dreams, unpregnant of my cause,
> And can say nothing—no, not for a king,
> Upon whose property and most dear life
> A damn'd defeat was made. Am I a coward?
> Who calls me villain, breaks my pate across,
> Plucks off my beard and blows it in my face,
> Tweaks me by the nose, gives me the lie i' th' throat
> As deep as to the lungs—who does me this?
> Ha!
> 'Swounds, I should take it: for it cannot be

But I am pigeon-liver'd and lack gall
To make oppression bitter.

(2.2.556–74)

The words rebound on the speaker. Who does him this?
Who but himself, in this very speech, reproaching himself
for lazy cowardice, and taking it, like a lazy coward. Must
Hamlet like a whore unpack his heart with words and fall
a-cursing like a very drab? He must, he does, he is. We
sense that he is self-stymied, his own opponent as profoundly as he is Claudius's.

The figure of Avenging Night is an ideal that keeps elud-
ing him, perhaps in part because it is contrary to his other
ideal, embodied in Horatio (more an antique Roman than
a Dane): "Give me that man / That is not fortune's slave"
(3.2.71). Even this speech must be cut off ("Something too
much of this") so that Horatio can be informed of the
Mousetrap stratagem. Both the ideals, as Gordon Braden
observes, both Avenging Night and the man immune to fortune, derive from Seneca.[21] In his drama we find blood and
horror, stages strewn with the calamities of unrestrained
passion. In his philosophy we find the precepts of a stoic
sage recommending apathy, the rigid control of internal
reality against the onslaughts of fortune. In the drama, the
man who in suffering all, suffers all; in the philosophy, the
man who in suffering all, suffers nothing. The two contrary
halves of this legacy descended to the Renaissance in separate traditions. It is part of the historical originality of *Hamlet* that the ethos of Senecan revenge tragedy should collide
in its hero's soul with the ethos of stoic indifference. Prior
to Shakespeare, the two Senecan traditions had rarely encountered each other.

This collision is precisely what we behold in "O what a rogue and peasant slave am I!" and the other speeches of self-reproach. Hamlet is rich in the vocabulary of insult, one of Shakespeare's specialties. He calls himself a rogue and peasant slave, a dull and muddy-mettled rascal, a John-a-dreams, a pigeon-livered coward, an ass, a drab, a scullion. But underlying this torrent of self-abuse, and the gallery of detested souls it generates, is this conviction: *I must be indifferent to my revenge.* Of course Hamlet does not consciously practice this stoic discipline. He would rather be Avenging Night. But the indifference is implicit in his cynical wit, his constant sense of superiority to those purposeful souls with whom he converses, and most of all in his self-reproaches. Shakespeare seeded his soul with a mysterious and unwilled allegiance to *apatheia.*

Sometimes the two ideals can join forces in the same decision. Thus Hamlet, on his way to his mother, comes upon Claudius at prayer. He could "do it pat," do it and be done with it. "And now I'll do it," he resolves, drawing his sword. But he will not strike the blow, not be passion's slave, not give up his melancholy distaste for all the uses of the world. And Avenging Night agrees, though for different reasons. It would not be revenge enough. Claudius must be damned, struck with a vengeance bearing the force of an angry god: "Up, sword, and know thou a more horrid hent" (3.3.88). So the revenge is put off into the future.[22] In this case, the cooperation of the two sides of the Senecan tradition produces delay.

The great closet scene, the climax of Act 3, opens with a turnabout. Hamlet has been informed by Rosencrantz to expect a dressing down: "Your behavior hath struck her into amazement and admiration" (3.2.317–18). Today the

word "behavior" in this context bespeaks parental authority, and Hamlet's ironic reply, "A wonderful son, that can
so stonish a mother," indicates that the same was true in
the Renaissance. Polonius expects Gertrude to "tax him
[Hamlet] home" (3.3.29). He thinks his own presence behind the arras will be necessary, not because Hamlet might
reveal secrets, but because nature makes mothers partial
and the presence of a father will encourage vehemence in
the queen's rebuke (3.3.29–34). What a purpose mistook,
then, falling on the inventor's head, when Hamlet charges
her with offence, refuses to let her leave, promises to reveal
her innermost sins, and by his own vehemence leads the
queen to think that he may intend to murder her. Echoing
her cry for help, Polonius is slain. Hamlet, deep in rashness,
does not even bother at first to address a single word to the
corpse. He has come with daggers in his tongue, and they
must be delivered.

Charging her with murder and marriage, he ascertains
her innocence of the first charge, but on the second count
Gertrude's heart proves permeable. "Thou turn'st my eyes
into my very soul, / And there I see such black and grained
spots / As will not leave their tinct" (3.4.89–91).[23] Though
it has been questioned, the stains seem pretty clearly those
of an adulteress: Hamlet's point in holding up the two pic-
tures is not simply that she married Claudius, but that she
preferred him when both were available. Three times Gertrude says she can endure no more dagger wounds: "O
speak to me no more," "No more, sweet Hamlet," "No
more." But Hamlet has not had enough, and continues
after the third "no more": "A king of shreds and patches — ,"
at which point the ghost appears. The obvious effect of the
timing is to indicate that he appears to make Hamlet obey

his mother and stab no more. Before the ghost can speak, Hamlet puts words in his mouth, assuming that the spirit has come to continue the business that he himself has been prosecuting of late, "your tardy son to chide / That, laps'd in time and passion, lets go by / Th'important acting of your dread command" (107–9).

The ghost's reply is a turning point:

> Do not forget. This visitation
> Is but to whet thy almost blunted purpose.
> But look, amazement on thy mother sits.
> O step between her and her fighting soul.
> Conceit in weakest bodies strongest works.
> Speak to her, Hamlet.
>
> (110–15)

The command to "step between her and her fighting soul" is either an addition to those given during his first visit or the clarification of a possible ambiguity. Earlier Hamlet was told not to contrive anything against his mother but "leave her to heaven, / And to those thorns that in her bosom lodge / To prick and sting her" (1.5.86–88). This might be interpreted in such a way that Hamlet is being perfectly obedient in his dagger-speak. The thorns are those of guilt and bad conscience. Hamlet has turned her gaze to the black spots on her soul: the pricking and the stinging, to which the ghost commanded she be left, are now begun. But, the ghost's appearance tells us, Hamlet *has* contrived a plot against his mother. His wounding words have left her broken and self-appalled; the remark about "conceit" implies that she may be close to taking her own life. Hamlet must intervene. First he was Avenging Night, then with "Soft, now to my mother" he halved his rage, vowing to speak murderous words but not commit matricide. Now the ghost has interrupted Hamlet with, in effect, a second "Soft," commanding him to remove the murderousness from his words.[24]

"How is it with you, lady?" Hamlet begins. The words come right back to haunt him. "Alas, how is't with you," she returns, unable to see or hear the ghost he has been attending to. After an interlude on the subject of Hamlet's madness, he revisits her spiritual condition, now more the minister than the scourge. The issue is her trespass, not his madness. She must confess, repent, mend her ways, "And . . . not spread compost on the weeds / To make them ranker" (153–54). He has retrieved the first soliloquy's metaphor of the world as a rank unweeded garden, but it soon appears that the recycled image is another of his notably disgusted expressions for sexual intercourse. The full plan surfaces in this extraordinary line: "Good night. But go not to my uncle's bed" (161).

On the one hand, we are reminded of the particular force of "good night" within the emotional economy of a family living under the same roof. I realize that servants and the protocols of a court would complicate these arrangements, but we know that Shakespeare's feeling for "good night" was formed in simpler circumstances. In the household of John and Mary Shakespeare, as in my own childhood, the earliest good-nights must have been exchanged at the place where the children slept; an older child might come to the bedroom of his parents for his daily sign-off. The ritual gradually accrues a history synonymous with growing up itself, as emotions and experiences are day by day funneled into the reliable sameness of "good night." All children are at some point frightened of the night. The "good night" of a parent is both reassuring (the daily round of family life will continue as it has in the past) and anxiety-producing (it signals departure, one's consignment to the dark). "But this good night," we read early in *Remembrance of Things Past*, "lasted for so short a time, she went down again so soon, that the moment in which I heard her climb the stairs . . . was for me a moment of the utmost pain, for it heralded the moment which was bound to follow it, when she would have left me and gone downstairs again."[25] On the part of parents, the exchange of good-nights reminds them of their protective function — of their duty, even as they temporarily abandon it.

But Hamlet's is a wild and whirling good-night, bursting with insinuation. There is, first of all, no exchange. Hamlet says "good night," yet his mother breaks linguistic convention by failing to close the circuit. It is not difficult to guess why. Gertrude is still reeling from an angry tongue-lashing, there is a corpse on the floor, and her son speaks to the air. Blithely undisturbed by these chaotic circumstances, Hamlet's good-night seizes parental authority. He has come to her, the role originally played by parents. He speaks for his father, condemning the behavior of his mother. "Good night" — I dismiss you, am about to leave you alone — "But go not to my uncle's bed." As he earlier suggested he would, Hamlet seeks to kill the incestuous marriage: "Go to, I'll no more on't, it hath made me mad. I say, we will have no more marriages: those that are married already, all but one, shall live" (3.1.148–49). This is a good-night of moral authority: I wish you a *good* night, a habit breaker, free of incest, the first and toughest in a sequence of good nights. Claudius, however, is to be deprived of "good night" in its sexual meaning.

"Good night," the ordinary signal of day's end, our separation from society, becomes a brilliantly transforming
refrain as the scene winds toward its close.[26] Shakespeare
has not attempted a drawn-out farewell of this intricacy
since the famous balcony scene of *Romeo and Juliet* with
its six good-nights (or 1,005, depending on how one counts
"A thousand times good night") capped by Juliet's "Good
night, good night. Parting is such sweet sorrow / That I
shall say good night till it be morrow" (2.2.185).

After the instructions about staying out of the king's
bed, "Once more, good night" (172). At long last Hamlet
consents to be adult about Polonius:

> for this same lord
> I do repent; but heaven hath pleas'd it so,
> To punish me with this and this with me,
> That I must be their scourge and minister.
> I will bestow him, and will answer well
> The death I gave him. So, again, good night.
>
> (174–79)

All kinds of moral seriousness have been read into these
lines, but they seem to me, rounded off by the scene's third
good-night, comic in a manner altogether unprecedented
in the history of drama.[27] Where he should be desperate,
Hamlet is placid and quotidian. His "So" links good-night
causally to his willingness to "answer well" for the murder
of Polonius. *Because* he will do the time, their good-night
can be an ordinary one, vouchsafing that the business of
the day is done, no loose ends remaining. "I will clean up
after myself," Hamlet assures her, "and this can be, after
all, just another good-night."

After more instructions about not yielding to sexual

temptation and not revealing to Claudius "that I essentially
am not in madness, / But mad in craft" (189–90), after promising that Rosencrantz and Guildenstern will be hoisted
with their own petards, Hamlet offers his final good-nights:

> This man shall set me packing.
> I'll lug the guts into the neighbor room.
> Mother, good night indeed. This counsellor
> Is now most still, most secret, and most grave,
> Who was in life a foolish prating knave.
> Come, sir, to draw toward an end with you.
> Good night, mother.
>
> (215–19)

Good night indeed! After the cosmic consequences of the
murder of Polonius have been faced, there remains the prac-
tical question of the corpse, how to move it and where to
put it. Hamlet chooses to lug it, not hoist it on his should-
ers, which must make the journey to the doorway a slow
one. There is time to taunt the corpse as he drags it across
the stage: Hamlet has acquired a possession, a toy designed
to hone his wits. The couplet rhyming "grave" and "knave"
would normally mark the end of the scene, but this is Hamlet wild and whirling, breaking all convention even as he
utters as bland a piece of ordinary language as English has
to offer. It follows as the night the day that all the changes
must be rung. He draws toward an end with Polonius, with
the day, with the presence of his mother. The scene cannot
end until "Mother, good night" is reversed to "Good night,
mother," the classic formulation no doubt, one of the deepest traces of filial tenderness. Tragedy is just another fact of
life. The greatest scene in *Hamlet*, the greatest of Shakespeare's plays, ends with a demonstration of the ordinary's

ability to survive anything. Is this madness? Is this supreme sanity? In this scene at least, Hamlet has risen above the distinction.

Such is not the case with Ophelia. She dies "as one incapable of her own distress" (4.7.177), her collage of old ballads suggesting a deep oedipal confusion between loss of a father and rejection by a male suitor. In her flowery gifts, Laertes observes, "Thought and affliction, passion, hell itself / She turns to favour and to prettiness" (4.6.185–86).[28] An aesthetic impulse, the urge to hang a garland on a limb, leads directly to her death. In this respect she repeats the pattern habitual with Hamlet, in whom the most ambitious and inspiring Renaissance ideas collapse into base conclusions: "What a piece of work is a man, how noble in reason, how infinite in faculties . . . and yet, to me, what is this quintessence of dust?" Precisely like man in this famous sentence, Ophelia climbs upward to beautify a bough but sinks in the end to "muddy death" (4.7.182).

Her good-nights have the same doubleness, expressing both an aesthetic aspiration and a failure:

> I hope all will be well. We must be patient. But I cannot choose but weep to think they would lay him i' th' cold ground. My brother shall know of it. And so I thank you for your good counsel. Come, my coach. Good night, ladies, good night. Sweet ladies, good night, good night. (4.5.68–73)

Coaches, imported from Holland by Elizabeth herself, the first owner of a coach in London, carried the entire city by the turn of the century, prompting some to complain that a plague of enormous squeaky insects had infested the streets.[29] Shakespeare's source is the raving Zabina in *Tam-*

burlaine, Part 1: "Hell, death, Tamburlaine, hell! Make ready my coach, my jewels, I come, I come, I come!"[30] Gone is the rage. Gone is the purposefulness of the journey. Ophelia calls for her coach, not to meet someone, but to go home at the end of an evening—metaphorically, to take leave of her senses, this life, the play, a traveller to "the undiscover'd country" (3.1.79). She is the only woman of Hamlet's generation, the only woman he might have loved and might have married. Her four good-nights are for the ladies, bearers of a sweetness Hamlet cannot recognize.

There remains the last and most moving good-night:

Hamlet.   O, I die, Horatio.
The potent poison quite o'ercrows my spirit.
I cannot live to hear the news from England,
But I do prophesy th'election lights
On Fortinbras. He has my dying voice.
So tell him, with th'occurrents more and less
Which have solicited—the rest is silence. [*Dies.*]
Horatio. Now cracks a noble heart. Good night, sweet
     prince,
And flights of angels sing thee to thy rest.

$$(5.2.357-65)$$

Again, in metaphor, the cock crows.[31] Hamlet has come to the last of his nocturnal fates. He has of course sought death from the first soliloquy onward. Now felicity is his, and his last breaths in this harsh world are drawn in silence. One must have a mind of night to behold the dark equipoise of the play. If we remember the very beginning of *Hamlet*, we see now that Horatio is the successor to Francisco. By bringing Hamlet news of the ghost, he sets in motion a story that he has almost nothing to do with, then at its end says good night. Good wishes complete the tale. Before telling Hamlet's story, Horatio quietly makes its last moment perfect, everything that life has not been. "Rest, rest, perturbed spirit" (1.5.190), Hamlet told his father's ghost, which was to say: "Rest, father, for I have taken on your cause, your restlessness." That fate still inheres in the silent and inclusive "rest," suggesting unfinished business, of his death speech. It is with Hamlet's turbulent fate sympathetically in mind that Horatio wishes him an everlasting "rest" free from the "bad dreams" of damnation that have troubled his soul: "For in that sleep of death what dreams may come, / When we have shuffled off this mortal coil, / Must give us pause." Due to her uncertain death, Ophelia was denied a funeral mass: "We should profane the service of the dead / To sing sage requiem and such rest to her / As to peace-parted souls" (5.1.229–31). Horatio immediately fills the "silence," Hamlet's dying word, with a requiem of angels, angels that Hamlet twice called to his aid on beholding the perturbed spirit of his father (1.4.39; 3.4.103–4). He gives the prince sweetness as well, tending already to his "wounded name" (349). If anyone in the course of the play has known a sweet Hamlet, it is Horatio.

In making "good night" into a farewell to the dead, Horatio turns the phrase in a new light. It no longer sends a person to solitude and sleep. It no longer hopes to put at bay the terrors of ordinary night. Now "good night" consigns Hamlet to another life, beyond the reach of human thought. The diurnal world of day and night disappears, replaced by the full Christian significance of the phrase.[32] The unseen night Hamlet has entered may be either the endless restless midnight of damnation or the endless noon of everlasting rest. "Good night" at play's conclusion is the hope of salvation—the first comment on the story Horatio lives to tell. In our memories we will always append that hope to the end of Hamlet's life, obedient to his own hard-won conviction: "There's a divinity that shapes our ends, / Rough-hew them how we will" (5.2.10–11).

It is high art to enrich the language in this manner, achieving poetry in the formulaic and structure from its repetition. If John Donne, said to be a great frequenter of plays in his youth, ever saw *Hamlet*, he must have marveled at Shakespeare's ability to exhibit treasures of meaning lying unnoticed in the oblivion of the everyday. Night as melancholy, grievous, haunted, vengeful, hellish: no stereotype has been left unexercised. "Good night" has been shown to be formal, intimate, poignant, comic, mad, unflappable, ordinary, sweet, and prayerful, a thing of childhood and a thing to be said at the end of a life. There is no horizon beyond "good night," nothing we can do or say or know. It contains, and ends, tragedy.

3 A Woman's a Two-Face

In Act 2 an "affrighted" (2.1.75) Ophelia seeks the counsel of her father. Hamlet has paid her a call:

> My lord, as I was sewing in my closet,
> Lord Hamlet, with his doublet all unbrac'd,
> No hat upon his head, his stockings foul'd,
> Ungarter'd and down-gyved to his ankle,
> Pale as his shirt, his knees knocking each other,
> And with a look so piteous in purport
> As if he had been loosed out of hell
> To speak of horrors, he comes before me.
>
> (78–84)

This has sometimes been thought a scam, an example of Hamlet making use of the antic disposition to gain a reputation for madness. Wilson Knight terms the idea a "perversion of commentary."[1] Surely there must be easier ways to feign craziness. If Hamlet is playing a game, it is a wild and compulsive one in which he acts the part of his father's ghost "loosed out of hell / To speak of horrors." As it turns out, he does not speak at all. The episode in Ophelia's closet is a dumb-show prologue to the great closet scene of Act 3.

Who is Ophelia in this bizarre game? To pose that question wordlessly is in fact the game's point:

> He took me by the wrist and held me hard.
> Then goes he to the length of all his arm,
> And with his other hand thus o'er his brow
> He falls to such perusal of my face
> As he would draw it. Long stay'd he so.
> At last, a little shaking of mine arm,
> And thrice his head thus waving up and down,
> He rais'd a sigh so piteous and profound
> As it did seem to shatter all his bulk
> And end his being. That done, he lets me go,
> And with his head over his shoulder turn'd
> He seem'd to find his way without his eyes,
> For out o' doors he went without their helps,
> And to the last bended their light on me.
>
> (87–100)

What does he see as he holds her hard, stares hard, and sighs as if to end his being?[2] Polonius interprets the weird visitor as a stricken lover: "What, have you given him any hard words of late?" He is wrong of course, though love is indeed somewhere in the picture.

An actor in his youth, Polonius is familiar with the stage convention of love at first sight. Perhaps Hamlet has come to stare again at the face whereon his love was born. As

Polonius builds his case, we will learn from a letter that this devotion had once declared itself indubitable:

> *Doubt thou the stars are fire,*
> *Doubt that the sun doth move,*
> *Doubt truth to be a liar,*
> *But never doubt I love.*
> O dear Ophelia, I am ill at these numbers. I have not art
> to reckon my groans. But that I love thee best, O most
> best, believe it. Adieu.
>> *Thine evermore, most dear lady, whilst this machine*
>> *is to him,*   Hamlet.
>>   (2.2.115–23)

The letter is written in the awareness of a Renaissance gender cliché about men: they are oath-breakers, and a woman cannot trust their love vows, especially in courtship.[3] In Act I both Laertes and Polonius instruct Ophelia on this matter. The author of the letter, presupposing this climate of opinion, wants above all to be believed. He really loves; his oath can be trusted. The letter seeks to fuse these truths, but in laying doubts to rest Hamlet simultaneously, like Descartes with his *cogito*, raises them.[4] It is often pointed out that most Elizabethans *could* doubt the sphere of fire and the movement of the sun about a stationary earth. As Donne would put it in a famous passage in the "First Anniversary": "The element of fire is quite put out; / The sunne is lost, and th'earth, and no man's wit / Can well direct him, where to looke for it" (207–9). It would seem to be more difficult to doubt (suspect or believe) that truth is not truth but instead a liar. If we suppose that Hamlet, no doubt as an aftermath of the ghost's revelations, now doubts his love—and bear in mind that the consequence of doubting love is to think truth may be a liar—we arrive at a first rough interpretation of his intense stare at Ophelia: her once truthful visage has now become infected with the possibility of being a truthful-seeming visage, the mask of a liar. In his mind the gender cliché has been transferred from men to women. Hamlet has the blues in the night. A woman's a two-face.

Hamlet does not think much of his powers as a lyricist, turning with relief to the more down-to-earth sorts of truthfulness possible in prose, yet the lyric genre is somewhere in the background of his fearsome visit to Ophelia's closet. He stares at her face as if he would draw it. In Shakespeare's own sonnets we find the close kinship between love poet and artist: "Mine eye hath played the painter and hath stelled / Thy beauty's form in table of my heart" (Sonnet 24). Intense attention to the female countenance is a hallmark of the sixteenth-century English lyric. Suits are received there with smiles or frowns. Beauty makes its home there. Those devotional journeys known as blazons start there. Metaphor's well is there. Poets staring at female faces see coral, marble, diamonds, pearls, rubies, stars, suns, storms, lightning, swords, hooks, bird traps, roses, cherries, fountains, springs, gardens, whatall. Scholars in my readership must forgive me here, for it is pointless to document ubiquity. Pick up any good anthology of Elizabethan verse and behold the faces: the whole genre is a prolonged *hommage* to the entrancements of face-gazing. It is easier to note instances where the tradition produces a novelty, since in this case the very power of the tradition renders variation unmistakable. Donne, for example, stares repeatedly at a female face that stares back at him, but he makes no effort to render its beauty in decorative metaphor; he instead sees maps, worlds, and himself staring back from her staring eye—highly intellectual metaphors for love conceived of as necessarily mutual. Hamlet has struck the male posture rendered immortal in the poetry of his age.

Yet he holds Ophelia hard and sighs as if it were his last breath. Robert Burton observed of love, "'Tis the sole object almost of Poetry, all our invention tends to it, all our songs."[5] The poetry of love is dying in this scene, to be succeeded by the violence, sarcasm, and melancholy of satire or epigram: "Frailty, thy name is woman" (1.2.146). Great ideas come to disillusioned ends in Hamlet's thinking. The splendor of creation is "but a foul and pestilent congregation of vapours" (2.2.302–3); man, angelic and even godlike, is but a "quintessence of dust" (2.2.308); the infinite spaces of the mind are made restless by "bad dreams" (2.2.256). Hamlet's billet-doux suggests that the root of this rampant skepticism, this potent poison of disillusionment that o'ercrows his spirit, lies in the wounded idea of woman.

Now Hamlet knows from the ghost just how frail and two-timing woman is. As Bradley suggested, the movement in Hamlet's mind from the corruption of Gertrude to the corruption of all women has the character of a faulty syllogism: "His whole mind is poisoned. He can never see Ophelia in the same light again: she is a woman, and his mother is a woman: if she mentions the word 'brief' to him, the answer drops from his lips like venom, 'as woman's love'" (101–2). Until it is too late, Hamlet never doubts the logic by which Ophelia is condemned for Gertrude's frailty—never doubts that truth is a liar. In this sense, too, Ophelia has two faces: Gertrude's and her own. That doubleness seems deeply germane to the crazy game Hamlet is playing in his visit to Ophelia. He is the ghost, and she is Gertrude, who "lives almost by his [Hamlet's] looks" (4.7.10). His dumb show implies that the ghost ought to visit frail womanhood, giving Gertrude the bad fright she deserves. Depending on the makeup, or rather depending on whether Ophelia wears makeup, he can verily see the two faces on her one face. "I have heard of your paintings well enough. God hath given you one face and you make yourself another" (3.1.144–46). This particular gender gripe bears some scrutiny.

Moral complaints about cosmetics are familiar in the prose of the English Renaissance, though quite rare outside of satire in the poetry, which mostly lives to praise woman, including her powers as an artificer. Both Jonson and Herrick discover models for poetic excellence in a woman's capacity to adorn herself.[6] Shakespeare is the only Elizabethan poet of stature to allow serious moralizing about cosmetics in his love poetry:

> For since each hand hath put on nature's power
> Fairing the foul with art's false borrowed face,
> Sweet beauty hath no name, no holy bower,
> But is profaned, if not lives in disgrace.
>
> (Sonnet 127)

It sounds as awful as the witchcraft in *Macbeth*! Through the centuries people keep charging Milton with misogyny, but he never once complains about cosmetics. To my knowledge, the condemnation of cosmetics in an extreme and deeply felt moral vocabulary holds true throughout Shakespeare, who never has a good word to say about face-painting. Perdita, for example, defends her neglect of the "bastard" gillyvors by reference to her revulsion for painted women: "No more than, were I painted, I would wish / This youth should say 'twere well, and only therefore / Desire to breed by me" (*WT* 4.4.101–3). "Certainly the limits of adorning and beautifying the body," Donne writes, "are not so narrow, so strict, as by some sour men they are sometimes conceived to be" (*Sermons* 5:302). Shakespeare appears to have been one of those sour men.

In the graveyard scene Hamlet proposes that the final human face, the skull beneath the skin, bears a profound lesson for women. It stops their giggling: "Now get you to my lady's chamber and tell her, let her paint an inch thick, to this favour she must come. Make her laugh at that" (5.1.186–89). Nor is Hamlet the only one in the play to invoke the moral paradigm of cosmetic duplicity. Polonius has delivered himself of some pieties about sugaring over the "devil himself" with "devotion's visage" (3.1.47–49); Claudius, struck by the morally resonant idea of a false face, speaks his guilt in an aside:

> How smart a lash that speech doth give my conscience.
> The harlot's cheek, beautied with plast'ring art,
> Is not more ugly to the thing that helps it
> Than is my deed to my most painted word.
> O heavy burden!
>
> (3.1.49–54)

The association of cosmetics with prostitutes is conventional, since they covered faces pocked from venereal disease with their "plast'ring art." Whorishness is never far away from complaints against cosmetics.

To have one God-given face, then to create another: this is precisely the sort of thing that pamphleteers on the lunatic fringes of Elizabethan Puritanism say about playacting.

"And if they write of histories that are known, as the life of Pompey, the martial affairs of Caesar, and other worthies, they give them a new face, and turn them out like counterfeits to show themselves on the stage." Actors are famously untrustworthy. "They have got such a custom of counterfeiting on the stage, that it is grown to a habit, and will not be left." "In stage plays for a boy to put on the attire, the gesture, the passions of a woman, for a mean person to take upon him the title of a Prince with counterfeit port and train, is by outward signs to show themselves otherwise than they are, and so within the compass of a lie."[7] Shakespeare, denouncer of cosmetic seeming, belongs to a profession that trades on this very art. We seem to be dealing with an area of his mind under no obligation to be made consistent with his other beliefs and practices.

I look to Freud for help. In the second essay of his *Three Contributions to the Psychology of Love*, variously known in English by the majestically ominous titles "On the Universal Tendency to Debasement in the Sphere of Love" and "The Most Prevalent Form of Degradation in Erotic Life," Freud considers why males cannot readily achieve an integrated vision of woman and must as a consequence cleave her image into idealized, spiritually lovable figures and debased, sexually desirable figures. This split has untold variations, but has come to be known by one of the most extreme, the virgin and the whore. In that extreme instance, the separation, the work of the split, is manifest. Because she cannot be a sexual object, the virgin can be idealized. Because she cannot be idealized, the whore can be a sexual object. Men have trouble getting love and desire to lie down together.

Freud traces the origins of the split to the male oedipus

complex. The fundamental task in splitting is to keep good and evil from cohabiting the same figure, in this case the mother. Internalized as goodness itself, as peace, happiness, and provision, the early mother is also destined to become the faithless woman of male fantasy. When a boy comes gradually to understand that not only animals have sexual intercourse but also people, and not only people but his very own parents, he feels that his mother has betrayed him. Her bond with the father spells the defeat of his first sexual venture. He may blame his unhappy desires, the entire oedipal sorrow, on her seductiveness. Although born of jealousy and frustration, there is relief of a kind in this misaccusation, for the vision of an unfaithful and betraying mother supplies him with a strategy for undoing in fantasies the incestuous attachment that binds his early love. The boy might, after all, possess his mother were she a *very* unfaithful woman, a woman available to any man: a whore. There being no question of love with such a woman, sexual fantasies cultivated about her can disguise their incestuous origins. On the other end of the scale, the figure of the virginal woman protects the goodness of the early mother from sexual contamination.

This is all quite abstract. To bring it into an initial alignment with our discussion of *Hamlet*, let's imagine a six-year-old boy whose mother has just said "good night," extinguished the light, and left him in the dark. The phrase so resonant in *Hamlet*, ending day, light, and society, also signals throughout psychic development the release of fantasy—unfettered fantasy, free from the impediments of day, light, and society. The boy is alone in the dark and wishes his mother were still with him. Where is she? She has gone, he thinks, to the bed she shares with his father. He wishes he were his father. For a moment he tries out wishing that she has gone to the bed of another man: a first sketchy attempt at the fantasy of the faithless woman. The fantasy has its pleasures. Now his father suffers the same fate he suffers, being alone at night. The boy can think of how happy that other man would be without envying his father, which is what happens when he thinks of where his mother really is. How could he get to be that other man? It is getting muddled. He is tired now, and thinks of something else, his wishes for tomorrow, as he falls asleep.

Let's imagine the same boy twice as old, now in the throes of puberty. For years, spared by the forgetfulness of latency, he has not had sexual thoughts, but now they are back. His mother says "good night." He retires to his bed. He blows out his candle or flips off his lights. He thinks of a girl across town, the one his friends say will do anything, or he thinks of the *Playboy* centerfold, open as a sexual fantasy to any man who can procure the magazine. He is aware of no hint of incest in these fantasies: oedipal repression has been successful, and the split has done its work. For these are not women like his mother, women he would court or marry. But the thought of them has just now given him an erection. I suspect that the physiological exclamation point of the male erection, which has no real analogue (at least in psychological terms) in women, sponsors male splitting. Because sexual arousal results in what is virtually a different physical condition, the boy imagines that there are women set aside from other women to satisfy the desires of this different animal. The boy masturbates. Depleted, vaguely guilty, but free from the tyranny of sexual compulsion, he falls asleep. What dreams may come? The nightmind endlessly ponders sexuality.

The toughest test for this male dualism is marriage. If woman at deep layers of the male mind is split into the ideal and the sexual, what is a wife? An anomaly, like a real mother. But if the heterosexual male is to achieve maturity, the images cut asunder in boyhood must now reunite. "A man shall leave his father and his mother," Freud writes, remembering the biblical command, "and shall cleave unto his wife; affection and sensuality are then reunited" (11: 181). The oedipus complex and its sequels are, in Freud's theory, the psychological results of having a father and a mother; marriage will not be successful unless a man can "leave" those attachments, fantasies, and divisions. Men begin with a real mother, but never know her until they find her again, in maturity, in a wife both loved and desired.

"In a wife I would desire," Blake writes, "What in whores is always found / The lineaments of Gratified Desire."[8] He says almost the same thing about a woman's desire in a husband. It ought to be a match. But Freud thinks that healing the split is a rare accomplishment in a man, because he "almost always feels his respect for the woman acting as a restriction on his sexual activity, and only develops full potency when he is with a debased sexual object; and this in its turn is partly caused by the entrance of perverse components into his sexual aims, which he does not venture to satisfy with a woman he respects" (185). Moreover, the universal tendency is toward degradation. Once sexuality is enjoyed, the idealization at the core of love stands in danger of collapse:

That ever holds: who riseth from a feast
With that keen appetite that he sits down?
Where is the horse that doth retread again

His tedious measures with the unbated fire
That he did pace them first?—all things that are,
Are with more spirit chased than enjoy'd.
How like a younger or a prodigal
The scarfed bark puts from her native bay—
Hugg'd and embraced by the strumpet wind!
How like the prodigal doth she return
With over-weather'd ribs and ragged sails—
Lean, rent, and beggar'd by the strumpet wind!

(MV 2.6.8–19)

Gratiano's examples, which might be multiplied forever ("that ever holds"), delineate an expressly sexual version of innocence and experience—enthusiastic chase followed by an aftermath of broken despair. In view of the tendency, Freud reasons, "an obstacle is required in order to heighten libido; and where natural resistances to satisfaction have not been sufficient men have at all times erected conventional ones so as to be able to enjoy love" (187).

The split itself may act as a barrier, heightening libido only to stymie it. For example, it would appear that the two female roles can be correlated with the superego (the virginal or virtuous) and the id (the sexual or lustful); but as Freud always stresses, the superego enters into unconscious alliance with the id (19:48–48, 51–52, 169–70). The net result of the split at its most severe is that a man cannot love where he takes pleasure or take pleasure where he loves. This must be the superego's touch: you can't *ever* get what you want.[9]

Every *Hamlet* critic in the psychoanalytic tradition has either argued or presupposed the crucial importance of this split in the characterization of the prince.[10] I am not breaking new ground, but I do have some new ideas about how to farm it. For one thing, the Freud-Jones reading of *Hamlet* attempts to solve a problem stemming from a prior and nonpsychoanalytic interpretation of the play: the great mystery in this tragedy is its hero's delay in achieving his revenge. As we saw in the first chapter, Freud's is a reading of the Romantic *Hamlet*. Given this initial take on the play, the psychoanalytic material of greatest moment concerns father and son.

Hamlet is self-thwarted because he is asked to kill a man who murdered his father and married his mother, the crime in the unconscious of every heterosexual male. "Use every man after his desert, and who shall scape whipping?" (2.2.524–25). At the heart of the mystery stands the doubling of Claudius and Hamlet.[11] Thus the hero veers from angry enunciations of forthcoming revenge to despairing analysis of the feasibility of suicide; if one assumes the doubling of Hamlet and Claudius, the acts would be equivalent. Thus "To be or not to be" remains, after the attentions of the cleverest critics in the world, an incoherent speech, because "enterprises of great pitch and moment" is an irreducibly odd way of referring to suicide, and should instead name something on the "to be" side of the equation, such as killing the king; but things straighten out if we assume that, given the doubling, it is perfectly natural for an argument against suicide to end with the impossibility of killing Claudius, "sicklied o'er with the pale cast of thought." Thus the language Hamlet uses to reproach Claudius tends to migrate into his self-reproaches, as when "O what a rogue and a pleasant slave am I!" thirty-two lines later becomes "I should ha' fatted all the region kites / With this slave's offal." Again, given the doubling, Hamlet's contempt for Claudius is the other side of his contempt for himself. Thus the Claudius figure in *The Murder of Gonzago* is Lucianus, nephew to the king. And so on, as details fall elegantly into line. I tip my hand: this seems to me much the best reading yet of the delay.

To be Bradleyan about it, Uncle Claudius must have been the "other man" in the earliest virgin/whore fantasies of young Hamlet. For in that fantastic case:

1. Hamlet himself made a whore of Gertrude by first imagining that Claudius made a whore of Gertrude. Now she actually does go to the bed of Claudius, originally the bed of King Hamlet. Both of them, one in fantasy and one in deed, have bewhored her.

2. In those early fantasies Hamlet and Claudius were rivals, but in the long run (in the fantasy construction of the woman available to all men) cohorts.

3. Hamlet substituted Claudius for his father. Claudius, doing the same thing, exposes the murderousness of that mental move. Fratricide is the twin of patricide.

Would this not account for Hamlet's conviction that his mother's recent marriage makes women into whores? His ambivalence as avenger? His indictment of Claudius proceeding alongside his indictment of himself? The killing of Claudius set against his killing of himself? Lucianus/Claudius, nephew to the king? I think so.

Yet, though not uninterested in the hero's procrastination, I have set myself another mystery: how are we to understand the Hamlet of Act 5, newly at peace with himself and in some fashion risen above his earlier self-thwartings? My bet is that the virgin/whore split, patiently followed, will shed light on this question. Before getting down to business, I must pause to discuss some guiding assumptions.

As in psychoanalysis itself, so in psychoanalytic readings of *Hamlet*, it has become fashionable to understand oedipal splitting as a relatively superficial revision of preoedipal splitting. Melanie Klein fired the starting gun, and now everyone runs from the dreaded pansexualist strain in Freud. Peter Erickson, for example: "As *Hamlet* dramatizes, men's sharply divided view of women as either chaste or sullied may be traced to a maternal base: behind the extremes of good and bad women lie the ideal and terrible mothers."[12] No doubt this is true, and there is some evidence that it might matter in *Hamlet*, though rather more in subsequent plays such as *Timon of Athens*, where sustenance comes into prominence first in banqueting, then in the withdrawn feast, then finally in discovering gold, "Thou common whore of mankind" (4.3.43), when digging for roots in mother earth. But I prefer to unfold *Hamlet*'s split on its oedipal or sexual level, which is the form in which it surfaces repeatedly in the text of the play.

In some distant way, yes, this split in Shakespeare's drama certainly reflects early traumas in the author's life. For me, hints elsewhere at the nature of those infantile revenge tragedies become clear in "Venus and Adonis," where the insistent embraces of Venus conjure up a breast being offered again and again to a satiate and increasingly alarmed baby.[13] My guess would be, to further tip my hand, that whoever breast-fed little Will (his mother, I'll wager) assumed that he would need much nourishment to survive infancy. As we know, two older sisters had not survived. About this nub a hundred plot turns, a thousand ways of putting things, eventually crystallize. Shakespeare's highest praise for love is that it does not cloy the appetite. Gertrude herself, Hamlet remembers, used to hang on King

Hamlet "as if increase of appetite had grown / By what it fed on" (1.2.144–45).[14]

There is also, in my view, a preoedipal foundation for the virgin/whore split in sibling rivalry, which for Shakespeare has its origins in being displaced at the breast by a new baby. It seems a good guess that Shakespeare was weaned at least nine months before his brother Gilbert arrived. Perhaps his long-nourished anger erupts in one of Timon's rants. He is asking Alcibiades to put Greeks to the sword:

> Strike me the counterfeit matron:
> It is her habit only that is honest,
> Herself's a bawd. Let not the virgin's cheek
> Make soft thy trenchant sword: for those milk-paps,
> That through the window-bars bore at men's eyes,
> Are not within the leaf of pity writ,
> But set them down horrible traitors.
>
> (4.3.114–20)

Timon places the false matron in conjunction with the virgin's milk-paps, "horrible traitors." The breasts are whores, he implies, because they will eventually suckle more than one child. We may also glimpse those traumatic early feedings in the way the milk-paps "bore."

Preoedipal interpretations always look "deeper." Their events happened first, their psychic patterns came into being first. But it is in the field of love and sexuality announced by the oedipus complex that this split makes its main contribution to Shakespearean drama. And that contribution is in turn a major one. There is no way to understand Hamlet, Othello, Posthumous, or Leontes without considering varieties of the virgin/whore split. Again I'll show my cards. I have said elsewhere that Milton is the great poet of the primal scene, the poet who gave that fantasy its most memorable workout.[15] Shakespeare is the great poet of the virgin/whore split.

A capacity to split well, to produce arresting divisions with ease and authority, cannot be other than a valuable trait in a dramatist, giving birth to exciting antagonisms (Richard III and the cursing queens, Coriolanus and Volumnia/Rome, Rome and Egypt in *Antony and Cleopatra*) and fascinating pairings of characters (lean Hal and fat Falstaff, Malvolio and the rest of Olivia's household, Othello and Iago, Ariel and Caliban). Shakespeare was drawn early in his career to the national divisions and redivisions of the Wars of the Roses, and the last play completely his was probably *Henry VIII*, chronicling the great schism in English religion. Around the time of *Hamlet* his style itself becomes richly double, turbulent with hendiadys or near hendiadys. The slicing and dicing of ideas observed at the level of style, in phrases such as "the perfume and suppliance of a minute," "the book and volume of my brain," or "enterprises of great pitch and moment," also occurs at the level of character and plot.[16] Not a Cornelius or a Rosencrantz, but Cornelius and Voltemand, Rosencrantz and Guildenstern: where one would suffice, we find two instead, hendiadys incarnate. The play itself exudes its own double in the play-within-the-play, and the play-within-the-play its own double in the dumb show. The incest Hamlet so abhors makes forbidden pairings in the positions of familial identification; Hamlet is the son-cousin of an uncle-father, and when off to England calls his father his mother since marriage has made them one flesh. This ubiquitous doubling, making one two and two one, has a kind of taxonomic beauty. Its sway over the smallest details of the tragedy, such as the repetition in "too too sullied" or "O God! God!" and the intense combination in the same speech of funeral and marriage, gives the victorious pleasure that successful literary formalism has always sought: the pattern is ours, open before us in a triumph of critical analysis. While not wishing for a moment to deny this pleasure, I do insist that the contemplation of the pattern cannot be a resting point for interpretation, since the splitting in *Hamlet* is instinct with drama — above all in the doubleness of woman.

Shakespeare's leading men do not as a rule crave degraded women. The most perverse sexual desire explored in his works is a soul-killing drive to ravish virtue: the satanic desire of Tarquin, Angelo, Iago, and Iachimo. When, in *Pericles*, Thaisa is marooned in a brothel, the bawd instructs her on the most profitable demeanor: "Mark me: you must seem to do that fearfully which you commit willingly; despise profit where you have not gain. To weep that you live as you do makes pity in your lovers: seldom but that pity begets you a good opinion, and that opinion a mere profit" (4.2.115–20). Ironically, she does this all too well, and produces the opposite effect, "able to freeze the god Priapus, and undo a whole generation" (4.6.3–4). Luckily for her there are no Angelos or Iachimos in Mytilene's brothel. The bawd's instructions lay bare the structures of sexual evil in Shakespearean males. They want recklessly to make virtue vice, virgins whores, chaste wives adulterous wives.

Understandably, the two faces of woman in the minds of Shakespeare's men have recently provoked a good deal of easy moralizing. I am not unsympathetic to the wrongs and injustices women have suffered, now as ever before, from this feature of the male psyche. As I have just indicated, some of Shakespeare's finest plays — *Hamlet* (in the fate of

Ophelia), *All's Well, Measure for Measure, Othello, Cymbeline, The Winter's Tale* — are palpably about those wrongs and injustices. But I do not believe, as moralizers seem to, that we will ever produce a generation of males from whom this split has been scrubbed away, however thoughtful and hygienic our parenting might become. The best we can hope for in this case is domestication. I regard the split as one of the supreme recurrent fantasies in our culture. To give a rough approximation, its domain stretches from the distinction between mint and cancelled in stamp collecting or cultivated plants and excluded weeds in gardening to the literary critic's division between original and derivative art. It gives shape to almost all of our best romantic plots, and if we were to delete from world cinema the romantic stories that turn on the difference between two women, or the possible two-sidedness of one woman, we would probably find ourselves with half as many movies. I furthermore think, showing all my cards, that our current academic culture of political correctness can be understood in psychological terms as a narcissistic denial of splitting. We are no longer to distinguish us from them, center from margin, lucid from confused, literary from nonliterary, great art from trivial art, sacred from profane, virgins from whores, nature from art, the unpainted from the painted face. What else is Derrida's attempt to find oppositions in which one term is privileged over another, then unravel them, but a head-on attack on splitting? All he can do, of course, is make new splits.

God is a god of long division. In the beginning there were splits. There will ever be splits. Splits are life. So I will not moralize about the two-faced woman in Hamlet's mind.[17] If the choice were between idealizing or condemning this psychic configuration, I would prefer to idealize it. The greatness of soul Hamlet ultimately achieves, like the literary greatness of Shakespearean drama, lives on its energies.

It seems to me that the virgin/whore split is especially primitive and vehement in English Renaissance males. We know that prostitution, like other rough amusements, was associated with the Bankside theatres.[18] For centuries brothels had been confined to this area; by venerable arrangement the Bishop of Winchester collected a tax on his "geese." The first serious attempt to break the terms of this ancient tolerance occurred under Henry VIII, who outlawed brothels in 1546. Although a couple of the old establishments remained in business, the result was that prostitution spread throughout the city. Taverns became fronts for whoring; to the chagrin of the London alderman, whores and pimps congregated around St. Paul's Cathedral. Then, too, the prostitution trade early on discovered an unforeseen advantage of the coach: they could do it in the road, which made their business at once flagrant and concealed, almost impossible to prosecute. Prostitution was newly visible in Elizabethan London.

It becomes a standard subject in Jacobean city comedy, where the adulterous turns of cornute husbands and bewhored wives tend to displace the comedy of courtship. Sometimes, through all the witticisms and insults, authors express the real horror of the business. A character in Dekker's *The Honest Whore*, Part 1, tells a prostitute that "the sin of many men / Is within you" (2.1.412–13).[19] Her body is a site of forbidden mixtures: "You'll let a Jew get you with Christian: / Be he a Moor, a Tartar, though his face / Look uglier than a dead man's skull" (424–26). In her future lies "liquorish damnation" (433), diseases, poverty, scorn:

"Whores will be rid to hell with golden bits" (429). Religious writers are also aware of prostitution's real sorrows. The pious Bishop Hall, imitating Christ, refuses to enjoy the public theater of whores being carted through the streets on their way to a date with the beadle's lash: "Let others rejoice in these public executions; let me pity the sins of others and be humbled under the sense of my own."[20]

But the fortunes of real prostitution cannot begin to explain the extraordinary place of whoring in English Renaissance invective. Whores are thought to be great cursers. But Englishmen imaginatively dispense their most feared curse, disease, in the most popular oath of the day: "a pox on" you, both your houses, your issue, whatever the curser wishes to contaminate.[21] It is clear at a glance that to call a woman a "whore" or "bawd" is not usually to call her a prostitute. Hamlets says that Claudius has "bewhor'd my mother" (5.2.64), his only possible motivation being that she received "traitorous gifts" (1.5.43).[22] Such words are prompted by any kind of sexual impropriety, indeed by almost any kind of moral impropriety—or just by the fact that women are women. Jonson makes the point succinctly:

To put out the word, whore, thou dost me woo,
Throughout my book. 'Troth put out woman too.[23]

Catholicism is denounced in the vocabulary of prostitution for its whorish devotion to religious images; Anglicans of all stripes identify the Pope with the Whore of Babylon (Rev. 17.1). John Taylor writes two poems called "A Whore," wit-games based on the following principle: how many people and things may be called a whore? Zeus made whores in his sexual adventures, Cleopatra was a whore, men are whores, Petrarchan adoration is whorish, the edict closing the stews created "private whores" (110). A book is a whore, since it lies with all for money: "For both of them, with a wet finger may / Be folded or unfolded, night or day" (113). A companion piece entitled "The Bawd" reverses the principle: how many people or things may a bawd be called? She's a stargazer (always on her back), a charitable institution, a rhetorician (sugaring the bitter), a musician (skilled at pricksongs), a poet, and so on. Though doggerel, the poems are interesting for their imaginative project. They envision an English language that will have need for only two nouns, whore and bawd, and seem typical of their day in receiving prostitution as in invitation to reinvent the world in its terms.

Many were the types of Una and Duessa in the age of the Virgin Queen. One of Dekker's characters maps the split onto the towering figures of the classical inheritance: "Compare them I pray, *compara Virgilium cum Homero*, compare virgins with harlots."[24] But as in the *Faerie Queene* itself, Duessa spawns multitudes. It used to be a cliché of linguistic anthropology that one could tell the Inuits lived in an arctic climate because their language had so many words for the varieties of snow. Here's a list of Elizabethan terms for a whore, almost all of which appear in Shakespeare: drab, bawd, punk, quean, trull, gamester, polecat, cockatrice, bitch, monkey, slut, strumpet, stale, harlot, pinnace, runnion, tib, doxy, nun of Venus, goose of Winchester, trug, dell, squirrel, bona roba, hackster, stale, ramp, and rabbit. Real prostitution, obviously, has tripped the mysterious sources of cultural invention. What happened to the city of London happens just as visibly in the English mind.

The Shakespeare play most attuned to the idea of a

world given over to varieties of prostitution is of course *Troilus and Cressida*. The three principals in the love plot take oaths in which they consent to their future as representative archetypes in the English language. Supreme among the similes of truthfulness, "'As true as Troilus' shall crown up the verse / And sanctify the numbers" (3.2.181–82). Should Cressida play him false, her name will rule the similes of falsehood: "Yea, let them say, to stick the heart of falsehood, / 'As false as Cressid'" (193–94). Pandarus, the deal maker, also consents to the future: "let all pitiful goers-between be called to the world's end after my name: call them all Pandars" (198–200). At the end of the play Pandarus bequeaths his diseases to an audience of panders and prostitutes. The play is about how misogyny, like a disease, first passed into the body of language. It takes virulent new forms in Elizabethan England, as we have seen, but the oldest pox still rages; in *Henry V*, for example, we hear of the "lazar kite of Cressid's kind" (2.1.76). Like an epidemiologist, Shakespeare traces the germ to its origins in *Troilus and Cressida*.

I conclude my chapter with a discussion of *Troilus* because this play, written close on the heels of *Hamlet*, contains a pattern repeated throughout the mature Shakespeare. Someone who has an ideal vested in a particular person (or persons, as in the case of Timon's friends) suffers disillusionment. The person is now seen as the opposite of the ideal. But the disillusionment cannot be confined to the particular. Instead, it becomes immediately global, the whole world ruined by a single instance of failure. This pattern has important consequences for our understanding of *Hamlet*.

Troilus is in some ways an anatomy of honor.[25] One of the two main roots of this concept, central to all of Shakespeare, lies in military heroism. In the Greek camp Ulysses tells the sulking Achilles that honor, if not refreshed by present achievement, will fade into oblivion (3.3.145–89). What have you done for me today? Honor is mere reputation, the sense usually given to the term by disapproving Renaissance moralists.[26] But honor has another meaning among its champions. The Trojan debate on the justice of the war turns on a distinction between honor as reputation and honor as intrinsic value or "affected merit" (2.2.61), a preciousness in the object answerable to the esteem in which it is held. At the end of the counsel, when Hector concedes that "'Tis a cause that hath no mean dependence / Upon our joint and several dignities" (2.3.193–94), he knows full well that the higher honor, the union of value and merit, cannot be theirs. Honor has split into a virgin and a war, and men at war can do without a cause "precious of itself" (2.2.56).

The other main locus of honor is sexual. Throughout the Renaissance honor marks a gender difference. While male honor is military and political and governs relationships of oath and service between men, female honor is exclusively sexual and domestic, the virginity of a maiden and the fidelity of a wife.[27] Female honor, in other words, is a cultural reaffirmation of the virgin/whore split: a woman either has it or does not; honor makes the difference. In Renaissance poetry we find attacks on female honor in the libertine tradition. It is a sham, a pretense, a value imposed by jealous men. Honor, Carew maintains in "A Rapture," is "but a Masquer, and the servile rout / Of baser subjects only, bend in vain / To the vast Idol."[28] But the very same poet writes two of the period's most beautiful stanzas on female honor as intrinsic merit rather than mere reputation:

O hapless sex! Unequal sway
  Of Partial Honour! Who may know
Rebels from subjects that obey,
  When malice can on vestals throw
Disgrace, and Fame fix high repute
On the close shameless prostitute?

Vain Honour! thou art but disguise,
  A cheating voice, a juggling art,
No judge of virtue, whose pure eyes
  Court her own image in the heart,
More pleased with her true figure there,
  Than her false echo in the ear.[29]

Only intrinsic honor, "precious of itself," can guard the difference between vestals and prostitutes. As the love plot of *Troilus and Cressida* demonstrates, the loss of affected merit in the sphere of sexuality is far less readily borne than its loss in the sphere of war.

Accompanied by Ulysses and Thersites, Troilus receives from eye and ear the living testimony of Cressida's falsehood. Ulysses makes him swear to be patient, and he tries to be, several times repeating his vow: "I will not be myself, nor have cognition / Of what I feel: I am all patience" (5.2.62–64). The belling chorus of Thersites represents the demands of impatience. For him, "a proof of strength she could not publish more / Unless she said 'My mind is now turn'd whore'" (112–13). The whole damn stage belongs to warmongers and whoremongers; Thersites stands for the cynical excess in misogyny that makes an unfaithful woman into a whore. But patience, Troilus's resistance to the pressure of this conclusion, generates a rising curve of peculiar mental states. We have the impression of a mind disintegrating in elaborate rationalizations to avoid admitting the plain truth that Cressida once vowed constant love to him and now plays him false with Diomedes.

Seeing is not believing; perhaps Cressida was not here (124). If she was here, then there must be two Cressidas:

> This she?—No, this is Diomed's Cressida.
> If beauty have a soul, this is not she;
> If souls guide vows, if vows be sanctimonies,
> If sanctimony be the god's delight,
> If there be rule in unity itself,
> This was not she.
>
> (136–40)

The stacked *if*s enumerate the general propositions that must be lost if this *was* she. Again, none of them entails the plain truth. His mind prepares itself for global disaster: if it was she, there is no "rule in unity itself"; Cressida will split into two separate creatures, faithful and false, mine and his, ideal and debased. Diomed has his movie, Troilus has his movie. He registers the incipiently split Cressida as simultaneously a self-division in his mind:

> This is not she. O madness of discourse,
> That cause sets up with and against itself!
> Bifold authority! where reason can revolt
> Without perdition, and loss assume all reason
> Without revolt. This is, and is not, Cressid.
> Within my soul there doth conduce a fight
> Of this strange nature, that a thing inseparate
> Divides more wider than the sky and earth;
> And yet the spacious breadth of this division
> Admits no orifex for a point as subtle

As Ariachne's broken woof to enter.
Instance, O instance! strong as Pluto's gates:
Cressid is mine, tied with the bonds of heaven.
Instance, O instance! strong as heaven itself:
The bonds of heaven are slipp'd, dissolv'd, and loos'd.

(141–55)

As an exploration of what might be termed the psychological metaphysics of splitting, this has no peer in world literature.[30] The division is both in the woman and in the man, and in neither realm can it be tolerated. The ordinary alliance of same and different having been shattered, thinking "doth conduce a fight." A "thing inseparate" becomes a yawning gap, and yet this "spacious breadth," remaining inseparate, has not hole enough for a subtle thread. Ariachne's thread? The famous crux invites postmodern comment, and has received it.[31] If a mistake, it is a fantastically lucky mistake—a word that puts two into one, then invites us to separate the two and choose one over the other, then upon reflection invites us to live in admiration with the (con)fusion. Shakespeare also places a good thread (Ariadne's, which gets Theseus out of trouble) and a bad thread (Arachne's, whose sexual sampler gets her into trouble) in the labyrinth of Ariachne. The chiasmus linking hell's strength with the good Cressida and heaven's strength with the bad is yet another masterful touch. Troilus at an impasse has all of Shakespeare's attention.

Why the fierce resistance to one Cressida, the same but different? Because the whole point of a split is not to contaminate goodness. Because this admission, permitting evil to touch Cressida, will undo an ancient separation:

Troilus. Let it not be believ'd for womanhood.
Think, we had mothers; do not give advantage
To stubborn critics, apt, without a theme
For depravation, to square the general sex
By Cressid's rule: rather, think this not Cressid.
Ulysses. What hath she done, prince, that can soil our
    mothers?
Troilus. Nothing at all, unless this were she.

(127–33)

As soon as evil predicates light on Cressida, the split will
come undone. Whoredom will prevail over chastity, sully-
ing the very essence (in the full philosophical sense: the universal) of womanhood with degradation.[32] Troilus looks
ahead to the role of Cressida in the forthcoming history of
misogyny. Ulysses, who does not fathom the global thinking to which other Shakespearean males are prone, wonders what Cressida has to do with mothers. Here Shakespeare leaves the ominous question of mothers undevel-
oped, but later in the canon, Posthumous will investigate
Troilus's thought. A conviction of womanhood's dishonor
annuls knowledge of the father:

            We are all bastards,
And that most venerable man, which I
Did call my father, was I know not where
When I was stamp'd.

(*Cym* 2.4.154–57)

The "other man" fantasy, pursued to the extremity of universal conviction, annihilates the family, degrading the
mother and placing the father in doubt.
    As it turns out, Troilus does not suffer the dark conse-

quences foretold in his transition from belief to disbelief. He curses "false Cressid," a first inscription of her name in the dishonor rolls of forthcoming infamy: "Let all untruths stand by thy stained name, / And they'll seem glorious" (5.3.178–79). But he is able to convert his disillusionment into martial *thymos*: "Hope of vengeance shall hide our inward woe" (5.10.31). It is precisely this simple channel between inward pain and violent action that Hamlet cannot open.

Hamlet resides in the forthcoming world of corrosive misogyny. Like Troilus, he is spared the agony of doubting his paternity, but the diseases that enter culture in *Troilus and Cressida* infect him. There is a habit, a naturalness to Hamlet's misogyny: Cressida has bred like Duessa; Hamlet speaks the tongue. He inherits the language of Thersites, and with it his satirist's eye for self-confirming proofs of a misogyny already settled in advance. But his misogyny does not, like the one threatening Troilus, begin in the beloved and extend to the mother. Just the opposite: learning misogyny from the living evidence of his mother, he must determine what that will mean with respect to his beloved. We see this process, I believe, when a disheveled, wordless, staring Hamlet visits Ophelia. He is announcing, and displaying, division. "I am the same yet different. Look at me! Look at *you*! You are the same yet different. O madness of discourse! Though my heart break, I must hold my tongue. I do not know how to resolve bifold authorities, the life I had and the life I have, but I think we are different, different." We see the conclusion of the process in the forthcoming rejection scene.

It might be instructive to reflect yet again on Milton's paradise:

> A wilderness of sweets, for Nature here
> Wanton'd as in her prime, and play'd at will
> Her Virgin Fancies, pouring forth more sweet,
> Wild above Rule or Art, enormous bliss.

Here is the reuniting Freud looks for in a good marriage,
the language of wantonness interacting with the language
of virginal purity. This fusion is felt throughout the characterization of Eve, even in her physical gestures:

> So spake our general Mother, and with eyes
> Of conjugal attraction unreprov'd,
> And meek surrender, half embracing lean'd
> On our first Father, half her swelling Breast
> Naked met his under the flowing Gold
> Of her loose tresses hid.
>
> (4.492–97)

50% embracing, 50% not; 50% barebreasted, 50% not. The
polarities of lust and modesty have achieved democratic
representation in the sexual life of Eden. Even there this balance proves precarious.

It is even more precarious in Shakespeare than in Milton.
In the play most resolved to unite the two faces of woman,
Antony and Cleopatra, the heroine must constantly claim
her greatness against accusations of whorishness. It is as if
she tries to embrace the charge and render it null by elevat-
ing whorishness to sublimity—but there are always more
charges. Contempt for sexual women, like the Nile, is se-
cretly fecund. Before her Egyptian performance of Roman
suicide, she encounters this contempt one more time in the
clown who brings the worms: "But truly, these same whoreson devils do the gods great harm in their women: for in

every ten that they make, the devils mar five" (5.2.274–76). 50% for the gods, 50% for the whoreson devils. As she strives to transform this split between women into a union of possibilities within a single woman, the men of the world count Unas and Duessas.

4 Hamlet's Virgin

It's the difference between day and night. A man loves. Many ideals, the very fact that there can be ideals, rest on the worthiness of this love. But after an ordeal of testing, his love is proved false. Anger and hatred strike at the betrayer in pulsating tirades. The world may be indicted; the very conditions of life as we know it, the seeds of things, may be threatened with rupture. Chaos is come again. Doubt and disillusionment rip through existence like tectonic plates gone to war. Children are disowned, wives killed or imprisoned, beloveds spurned, mothers loathed, fathers rendered unknowable. Shakespeare does many things well, but immense — today we would say excessive — moral revulsion is a favorite inspiration in the tragedies and romances. This pattern of a lost faith followed by global disillusionment shapes most of the plays written after *Hamlet*. Shakespeare's drama elongates Donne's condensed "spider love, which transubstantiates all, / And can convert Manna to gall."[1]

But *Hamlet* itself inverts the pattern. Disillusionment has taken place, and its effects felt, as the play begins. The prince in his first soliloquy curses his sullied flesh, wishes to die, and detests the world. One sees traces of what might have been a Troilus-like "is and is not" response to his mother's hasty marriage in the repetition of "a month," "a little month," as if his mind were still getting used to that one. However spectacular and terrifying, the ghost's visit only adds fuel to the flames in informing him that his "virtuous-seeming" mother is in fact an exemplar of female lust, which will leave the "celestial bed" of a "radiant angel" to "prey on garbage." But all of this is in Act 1. One might argue that Hamlet does not completely and unequivocally trust the ghost until after The Mousetrap. It seems clear, however, that the mental damage has already been done; seeing Claudius blanch at the play changes none of his feelings about his stepfather, mother, or the world in general. Othello is far gone in disillusionment by Act 3 (though he does not get the handkerchief proof until Act 4); Lear hits the bottom in Act 4, then another bottom in Act 5; Timon stages his banquet of rage at the end of Act 3. What is elsewhere the dramatic crisis is in *Hamlet* almost a *donnée.*

The tragedies with the disillusionment pattern generate drama from a detailed study of the ideal's fall (*Othello*) or a gradual revelation of the depth of the consequences (*Lear*). Near the end, the hero may reconstitute a new ideal—Othello's defense of his love, Lear's reunion with Cordelia—but these late recoveries either add poignance to the loss or are themselves swallowed up in an overwhelming impression of loss. As a revenge tragedy, *Hamlet*'s central focus is on when and how the hero will fulfill his father's

task. But the delay makes room for another and more difficult achievement that in Act 5 ultimately absorbs the vengeance motive itself. In its thoroughness and dramatic exten-
sion, this achievement has no precedent in Shakespearean
tragedy. Out of a "flat" world overrun by "things gross in
nature" Hamlet, reversing the disillusionment pattern, will
make a complex ideal.

I do not mean to suggest that Hamlet is without ideals.
There is the quasi-divine figure of his dead father. There is
Horatio and the stoic imperturbability he exemplifies.
There is Pyrrhus, the persona of Avenging Night. There is
the well-acted play, "whose end, both at the first and now,
was and is to hold as 'twere a mirror up to the nature; to
show virtue her feature, scorn her own image, and the very
age and body of the time his form and pressure" (3.1.21–24).
But the phrasing of this last ideal can serve to remind us
that all of them are masculine: though art holding up a mirror to nature was conventional to the point of commonplace, Hamlet's version strongly evokes the correction of
female vanity. The undiscerning lust of his mother contam-
inates women, marriage, sexuality, conception, and flesh
itself. "It is the 'couch for luxury and damned incest,'"
Dover Wilson writes, "far more than the murder that transforms his imagination into 'as foul as Vulcan's stithy.'"[2]
Hamlet's efforts to make an ideal center on modifying or
escaping this disillusionment.

I begin with the rejection scene. Polonius and Claudius
have taken positions of concealment. Hamlet has just
finished the most famous speech in English drama. The cur-
rents have gone awry and the name of action has been lost.
Ophelia comes into view reading a devotional book. She

has something in her hand. Hamlet must shift from deep privacy to conversation:

> Soft you now,
> The fair Ophelia! Nymph, in thy orisons
> Be all my sins remember'd.
>
> (3.1.88–90)

Dover Wilson thinks the tone sarcastic here; Dr. Johnson, with Jenkins on his side, hears gravity and solemnity. Throughout the scene our judgment of tone is crucial. The Hamlet of Ophelia's portion of 3.1 can be played in attitudes ranging from anger to near tenderness. Some readers think Hamlet is trying to remove Ophelia from the scene of the forthcoming tragedy. Others think he knows she is being manipulated by Claudius and Polonius, and wishes to disentangle her from all the plots now set in motion by sending her to a nunnery. Still others feel that he is too angry at women to have much in mind beyond hurting his ex-girlfriend. So the tone of this opening line is consequential.

I line up with Johnson on the orisons because, "To be or not to be" still ringing in our ears, Hamlet's use of the term "sins" names something loudly absent from the soliloquy. There he lists the evils of life as ills we bear and shocks that flesh is heir to. Evil seems wholly external, and the turning point of the speech, the "rub" that deflects Hamlet's thoughts from the happiness of death to "the respect / That makes calamity of so long life," must be inferred by the audience:

> To sleep, perchance to dream—ay, there's the rub:
> For in that sleep of death what dreams may come,

When we have shuffled off this mortal coil,
Must give us pause —

(3.1.65–68)

Presumably "what dreams may come" alludes to the after-life. There would be no reason to dread such dreams unless Hamlet were imagining an afterlife of punishment, and no reason to imagine punishment unless he were guilty of sins. But how deep in inference these sins lie! The whole speech, in fact, is a strangely irreligious consideration of why we do not commit a sin, that of suicide.[3] Hamlet conceded in the first soliloquy that the Everlasting has "fix'd / His canon 'gainst self-slaughter." Now he has reasoned about whether one might do it anyway, only to hit the wall of divine decree. It cannot be gotten around. If he leaves the evils of his life in an evil fashion, he will suffer evils in the next life. The subjunctive "what dreams *may* come," combined with the deep inferential burial of sins, indicate a degree of skepticism. So I think "Nymph, in thy orisons / Be all my sins remember'd" is indeed grave and solemn, the words of a man who has flirted with skeptical self-determination but, pulled back by the dread of God, now submits to divine judgment in an almost Pascalian frame of mind.[4]

But I hear bitter sarcasm in "The fair Ophelia!" It was, after all, the summary site of this fairness, her countenance, that Hamlet visited her closet to hold before him and stare at closely. As this scene unfolds, we will learn that *fair* is a highly charged word for Hamlet.

Obeying her instructions, Ophelia returns his "remembrances." Hamlet first denies giving her anything: "No, not I. / I never gave you aught" (95–96). Metrical ictus puts a telling spin on the first "I" that probably passes to the second: Not *I, I* never gave you aught. He is announcing in words what the wordless visit conveyed. He is different now. As he says more conventionally later in the scene, "I did love you once" (115). Women, love, sweetness, gifts, and marriage are no longer for him. Ophelia is twice unsuccessful at handing back the packet ("I pray you now receive them," "Take these again"), and in the end seems to force it into his hands ("There, my lord"). His letters and tokens, the life of another Hamlet, a man who wanted above all to be believed in his love suit, now rest in his hands—the ocular proof that his suit is not believed. Ophelia's rejection might once have devastated him, but that was in another Elsinore, and besides the man is dead. Ironic laughter at the difference in himself kicks off another episode of wildness:

> *Hamlet.* Ha, ha! Are you honest?
> *Ophelia.* My lord?
> *Hamlet.* Are you fair?
> *Ophelia.* What means your lordship?
> *Hamlet.* That if you be honest and fair, your honesty should admit no discourse to your beauty.
> *Ophelia.* Could beauty, my lord, have better commerce than with honesty?
> *Hamlet.* Ay, truly, for the power of beauty will sooner transform honesty from what it is to a bawd than the force of honesty can translate beauty into his likeness. This was sometime a paradox, but now the time gives it proof. I did love you once.
>
> (103–15)

"Ha, ha!" turns the scene to prose, and the first thing that the new wild Hamlet wants to talk about is the sad contemporary state of the virgin/whore split. We now can be pretty certain that "The fair Ophelia!" was sarcastic. *Fair* stands for the whorish side of woman, while *honesty* stands for the virginal side.[5] The time gives it proof—Gertrude gives it proof—that the bad fair must corrupt the good honest.[6]

But, as in the case of Troilus, though with less philosophical rigor, the split inhabits a space in-between man and woman. It takes two to make an honest woman a bawd. There are Claudiuses in the world, and something of Claudius in all men, Hamlet included: "You should not have believed me; for virtue cannot so inoculate our old stock but we shall relish of it. I loved you not" (117–19). Doing unto Ophelia what Gertrude has done unto him, Hamlet serves as her disillusioner about the opposite sex. Sin is original in men as well as women. Virtue in men, like honesty in women, cannot escape the rank unweeded garden of a fallen world. As an example of how little men can be trusted, he denies the past love he has just affirmed. Love is on, then off, in the rhythm of the scene, which is reminiscent of the game played with flower petals. I never gave you aught. I did love you once. I loved you not. Hamlet seems at an impasse, spinning his wheels.

We must always bear in mind the pattern when reading Renaissance literature. Shakespeare's play with *yes* and *no* and a variety of other contraries (solemn/sarcastic, fair/honest, virtue/sin, nun/breeder of sinners) pervades the scene.[7] As in *Troilus* and *King Lear,* he is experimenting with a drama of splitting. If the pattern holds, the next declaration to Ophelia should be on the side of past love.

Hamlet proceeds to give her in a wild and extreme form the same lesson that Laertes and Polonius have urged on her. Men are not honest. The lecture begins with the scene's signature line:

Get thee to a nunnery. Why, wouldst thou be a breeder of sinners? I am myself indifferent honest, but yet I could accuse me of such things that it were better my mother had not borne me. I am very proud, revengeful, ambitious, with more offences at my beck than I have thoughts to put them in, imagination to give them shape, or time to act them in. What should such fellows as I do crawling between earth and heaven? We are arrant knaves all, believe none of us. Go thy ways to a nunnery. Where's your father? (121-32)

Between the two injunctions to go to a nunnery, Hamlet presents a fairly exhaustive revelation of his new selfhood. The strain of self-accusation is loud and clear. He shows her his desire to be Avenging Night, but in such a form—not enough thoughts, imagination, or time—as to betray the paralysis he feels. Life is purposeless and corrupt. "I could accuse me of such things that it were better my mother had not borne me" exposes one of his deepest ambivalences. The statement has a "to be" meaning (it were better that his mother had not borne him because he intends to hurt her and Claudius) and a "not to be" meaning (it were better not to be born, not to have to discover that there is no safe escape from sullied flesh and the ills it must bear). Once concerned to be believed as a lover, he is now just as insistent on not being believed. The new self repeats in negative the gestures of the old.

Students refer to this as the "'Get thee to a nunnery' scene"—and that is in truth where the action is. Hamlet's four repetitions of his chosen refrain vary the verb from *get* to *go*. As so often, the OED is instructive. Instransitive *get* means "to succeed in coming or going to, from, into, out of," and *go* is simply the "verb of motion, expressing a movement irrespective of the point of departure or destination": in his "sole commandment" Hamlet literally finds the name of action. This declaration *does* fall on the side of past love. He cared for her enough to direct her out of the marketplace of marriage. The injunction to be quick on the get-go is tender as well as angry. He can do nothing but crawl along with his negatives, delaying. She, on the other hand, might get and go, renouncing the world of marriage and entering a nunnery, where physical fairness counts for nothing. She has not been visited by a ghost. She has available to her a choice, a way out, that is world-rejecting but not suicidal. She can be (a nun) and not be (a breeder of sinners). Facing a whorish world without ideals, Hamlet tries to make a virgin.

It has long been debated whether the whorish sense of "nunnery" = s "brothel," derived from "whore" = s "nun of Venus," belongs to the intentions of the scene. Certainly the virginal sense is paramount. He is not telling her to get herself to a whorehouse. But with four repetitions it seems plausible that the audience would have heard the evil half of this definitively split word. In my view the power of the scene depends on the backdrop of prostitution. Out of this stew of corruption in Hamlet's mind emerges the possibility of an ideal woman. The corrupt sense still hangs about the virtuous, for Hamlet cannot so innoculate our old stock of words but they shall relish of it. When Gertrude remarried, the split collapsed into "Frailty, thy name is woman!" What is there to do but make the split again, and out of lustful frailty retrieve honor and honesty?

The to-and-fro between man and woman, his sins and her sins, continues. Hamlet's first reason for getting to a nunnery stems from the sins of men, the second from the sins of women. In another lingering farewell, anticipating the closet scene with Gertrude, Hamlet finds time to explore both sides of the question.

> *Hamlet.* If thou dost marry, I'll give thee this plague as a dowry: be thou as chaste as ice, as pure as snow, thou shalt not escape calumny. Get thee to a nunnery, farewell. Or if thou wilt needs marry, marry a fool; for wise men know well enough what monsters you make of them. To a nunnery, go — and quickly too. Farewell.
> *Ophelia.* Heavenly powers, restore him.
> *Hamlet.* I have heard of your paintings well enough. God hath given you one face and you make yourselves another. You jig and amble, and you lisp, you nickname God's creatures, and make your wantonness your ignorance. Go to, I'll no more on't, it hath made me mad. I say we will have no mo marriage. Those that are married already — all but one — shall live; the rest shall keep as they are. To a nunnery, go.
>
> (136–51)

The calumny inspired by the virgin/whore split seems at first a trumped-up charge, born of male misogyny, then a just accusation motivated by a wife's fooling around. This second possibility inspires a bout of woman-baiting: *you* in "God hath given you one face" surely means "you women." The godless superficialities of the sex drive him mad. The "fair" face of a woman is whorish, and so is her painted one. A conviction of universal female dishonor drives him to impatience. Yet he continues, as the impatience grows, to point toward his ideal. Wherever the split is, in men or in women, a matter of valuing or a matter of affected merit, she can escape in a nunnery; and Hamlet exits on "go," the imperative of action. His earlier "go to" means "come, come," get on with it: *go*.[8] In his mind, the possibility of a feminine ideal is threatened every moment with destruction. The exiting "go" brilliantly summarizes the confusion throughout about the locus of the threat: I can no longer stand to be in your presence, you should no longer be able to stand my presence.

To study the fate of this new ideal, we must revisit the closet scene. Hamlet cannot salvage purity from wrecked femininity without confronting its source, and he will bring to his audience with Gertrude the same jarring combination of anger and incipient idealism we have just observed in the rejection scene. But between the encounters with Ophelia and Gertrude lies the assembly of the play-within-the-play. The purpose is to catch the conscience of the king, but his repartee suggests that womanhood preoccupies the prince. The ideal trumpeted during the rejection scene, no doubt extreme and unrealistic to begin with, Hamlet now systematically destroys. Meanness poses as merriment, misogyny as humor.[9] Our memory of "Get thee to a nunnery," however, elevates the cruelty by transforming it into another of the character's mysterious spectacles of self-destruction. He who commanded her to leave a corrupt world now calls her to vulgarity and insult. But why? To act out in the presence of his uncomprehending mother the degradations she has visited on him? Because the prince seems at once deliberate and compelled, the sexual badinage during The Mousetrap rises to a peculiar sublimity of spite.

The question of where he will sit, posed by Gertrude, leads him inexorably to Ophelia's vagina:

Queen. Come hither, my dear Hamlet, sit by me.
Hamlet. No, good mother, here's metal more attractive.
[*Turns to Ophelia*]
Polonius. [*aside to the King*] O ho! do you mark that?
Hamlet. [*lying down at Ophelia's feet*] Lady, shall I lie in your lap?
Ophelia. No, my lord.
Hamlet. I mean, my head upon your lap.
Ophelia. Ay, my lord.
Hamlet. Do you think I meant country matters?
Ophelia. I think nothing, my Lord.
Hamlet. That's a fair thought to lie between maids' legs.
Ophelia. You are merry, my lord.
Hamlet. Who, I?
Ophelia. Ay, my lord.
Hamlet. O God, your only jig-maker. What should a man do but be merry? For look you how cheerfully my mother looks and my father died within's two hours.
Ophelia. Nay, 'tis twice two months, my lord.
Hamlet. So long? Nay then, let the devil wear black, for I'll have a suit of sables. O heavens, die two months ago and not forgotten yet!

(3.2.107–29)

As Hamlet turns from Gertrude to the more magnetic Ophelia, we seem for a moment to have dropped into one of Touchstone's scenes in *As You Like It*. But this is caustic merriment, "poison in jest" (229), meant in some measure to accuse the intolerable cheer of his mother.

Since editors have never fully explicated this passage, we must be at once careful and fearless. The witticism of "That's a fair thought to lie between maids' legs" is pro-

duced by the idea she might "think" he meant country matters (matters pertaining to the cunt) when asking if he could
"lie" on her lap. His strategy is of a piece with much of his
mad talk: if you understand me, you in effect reveal an oc-
cluded guilt. Ophelia tries to say that she was innocent of
the thought of country matters. "I think nothing, my lord,"
she maintains, clearly not intending the sexual sense of
"nothing" = s "vagina." Yet the word has that sense, and in
Hamlet's equivocating mind her declaration of innocence
convicts her.

So, in a little triumph of wit that gathers the strands of
"think," "lie," and "lap" in a single statement, Hamlet
delivers his best line so far. "That's a fair thought to lie
between maids' legs." One meaning seems to be: the thought
of lying between a maids' legs is a fair one to me — a forth-
right declaration of desire. But I cannot believe this the pri-
mary sense. It seems unlikely that Hamlet at this point
should express a sexual desire for Ophelia so simple and
abstract that it might define heterosexuality itself. The crucial notion is that the thought of "nothing" lies, is somehow located, between maids' legs. Here is the best I can do:
your cunt thinks nothing, which is to say, thinks itself, so
that when you think "nothing," as you just have, you and
your cunt are one. In the rejection scene we found the same
hesitancy over the location of thoughts concerning sinful
women. Does the "thought" of "nothing" lie in Ophelia or
Hamlet, woman or man?

Passages of this kind are common enough in Shakespeare. When he is writing in this manner, the very language itself seems under the sway of a universal tendency
toward degradation, as words repeatedly find their way to
the sexual organs, copulation, pregnancy, venereal disease,

prostitution, cuckoldry. The tennis masters playing sets of wit in Shakespeare generally enjoy themselves. There's sport in it. But Ophelia is not playing, though she seems to be appreciative. And Hamlet's merriment fairly quivers with cynical ferocity. A "fair" thought? We know from the rejection scene what the word "fair" has come to imply: that's a whorish thought to lie between maids' legs, corrupting honest chastity. Despite the apparent intimacy of the scene, Ophelia is just an instance of abstract womanhood for Hamlet, a target of taunting insinuations. "O God, your only jig-maker." How stupid she is, how little she understands! All women think about is nothing! "My father died within two hours," followed by the halving of "twice two months," suggests the immediacy for him of the play's representation. It takes him right back to the adultery, the murder, and the remarriage, a triad of rotten deeds that seem in his memory to have happened virtually at once.

Hamlet is lying down at Ophelia's feet. His posture has been related both to affected gallantry and tempted virtue.[10] Neither seems quite to fit this particular occasion. Perhaps we should stick to the obvious: he has become half as tall as she, and put his busy mind in proximity to the center of her body. Right next to his brain, as he watches the play and interprets for the rest of the audience, is a woman's sexual parts. He never forgets it. After the dumb show, which ends with the seduction of the Player Queen, a presenter takes the stage. Ophelia wonders if he will divulge what the show meant. "Ay, or any show that you will show him. Be not you ashamed to show, he'll not shame to tell you what it means." "Show" puns on "shoe," again the vagina: the theatrical show is to reveal the shame of the sexual show, and Hamlet again brings the shame home to the place of feminine sexuality next to his mind. The entrance of Lucianus carries these allusions to their foreordained end:

> *Ophelia.* You are as good as a chorus, my lord.
> *Hamlet.* I could interpret between you and your love if I could see the puppets dallying.
> *Ophelia.* You are keen, my lord, you are keen.
> *Hamlet.* It would cost you a groaning to take off my edge.
> *Ophelia.* Still better, and worse.
> *Hamlet.* So you mis-take your husbands.
>
> Begin, murderer.
>
> (240–49)

It would appear to be a turn-on to preside at a festivity demonstrating that your mother is a whore.

Wit first manufactures a sexual life for the virginal Ophelia. If he could see the shameless love acts she normally keeps hidden as he now sees the play before him, he could "interpret" them. Ophelia praises his keen wit. Hamlet then transforms a blade into an erection; it would cost her a groaning, the loss of virginity, to blunt his edge. His wit-thrusts at Ophelia's vagina have finally adduced a graphic evocation of their copulation. Appreciating all this as a performance in witsmanship, Ophelia is gracious. "Still better" (a better joke), "and worse" (a dirtier and more personal joke, aimed directly at her honor). Hamlet has a topper: "So you mis-take your husbands," where "you" again means "you women." In the marriage ceremony husbands are taken "for better for worse," but in Hamlet's misogynistic temperament, mistakenly taken. Wives are false to their vows. "Better" and "worse" returns this wit game to its buried presupposition, Hamlet's inability to maintain a split image of woman. Even in the women they chose to marry, men get the worse rather than the better. The sequence of witticisms follows the plot of the virgin/whore split with Ophelia in the role of Gertrude: first the thought that Ophelia is having sex with another man; then the thought that he might also possess her; then the thought of betrayed husbands, with wifely falsehood confessed in the "better" and "worse" of the marriage vow. Ophelia's innocent words enter the channels of Hamlet's soiled brain and reemerge in degraded images.

Clearly Sister Ophelia was not a feminine ideal with much future. If she can find entertainment in these insults, so be it. Catching the conscience of the king is no doubt the serious business here, the job the genre demands; but as he waits for that moment Hamlet's great pleasure is to act as debunking chorus to the dumb shows, puppet shows, and tragedies of female falseness. Ophelia will do in that kind. Yet Gertrude is the woman with whom he must speak. "Madame, how like you this play?" He brings her the play, *his* Mousetrap, in the closet scene.

Initially the scene calls attention to a split in the image of the father, as Hamlet juxtaposes the picture of a god among men with the picture of a beast among men. In Janet Adelman's powerfully schematic discussion of the play, male success depends on the clarity of this division: "The *Henry IV* plays and *Julius Caesar* both strikingly represent the defining act of the son's manhood as the process of choosing between two fathers; in both, the son attempts to become fully himself by identifying with the true father rather than the false, an identification signaled by the son's willingness to carry out the true father's wish that the false father be disowned or killed."[11] Hal's choice between

Henry and Falstaff (though it is less a choice than "a skill" in the terms of *1H4* 1.2.196–217) fits the generalization. To say that Brutus chooses between two fathers, his ancestor Junius Brutus and Julius Caesar, seems more of a stretch. But for the sake of the schema I proceed. This pattern is complicated in *Hamlet* by Gertrude's marriage to Claudius, which blurs the difference between true and false fathers (12–13). Thus Hamlet is insistent to the point of hysteria that she admit the many obvious distinctions between her two kings. Gertrude has scrambled the binary of manhood.

Adelman is right to detect some degree of cognitive dissonance in Hamlet's apprehension of father figures. Gertrude *must* know the difference; nature always supplies "some quantity of choice / To serve in such a difference" (3.4.75–76). But I would put the point less abstractly, nearer the earth of the text. Hamlet wants confirmation of the ghost's revelations. The Mousetrap plot has given him some, but the ultimate confirmation must come from Gertrude. No one else in this world can guarantee that his paternal ideals and debasements rest on the foundation of intrinsic merit. Gertrude must be reclaimed for the original Hamlet family, and all three of them, father, mother, and son, united against Claudius.

Her endorsement of the difference would, moreover, produce the needed split in Gertrude. As he directs her gaze to the "counterfeit presentment of two brothers" (54), he also stares at her, reopening the mysteries of the female face. "Have you eyes?" "Shame, where is thy blush?" His very image for her crime is the face of a modest and innocently loving woman branded a prostitute: "Such an act / That blurs the grace and blush of modesty, / Calls virtue hypocrite, takes off the rose / From the fair forehead of an innocent love / And sets a blister there" (40–44).[12] Her mistake in judgment, her inability to see the difference, must result from a prostitution of the mind: "reason panders will" (88).[13] The situation of degraded reason arranging trysts for the lustful will demands the old Trojan language, misogyny's myth of origins.[14] Immediately after hearing this phrase, Gertrude confesses to her "black and grained spots." Hamlet brings the language of prostitution home to its source, and finds that there is reason, and shame, and difference, after all.

There remains the extraction of pure chastity:

Queen. O Hamlet, thou hast cleft my heart in twain.
Hamlet. O throw away the worser part of it
And live the purer with the other half.
Good night. But go not to my uncle's bed.

(158–61)

His spoken daggers have cut her heart in two. By throwing away the worser half Gertrude can end the incest, void her marriage, renew her loyalty to King Hamlet, and regain a symbolic virginity. All the whorishness and degradation in the world are concentrated in that bed:

Nay, but to live
In the rank sweat of an enseamed bed,
Stew'd in corruption, honeying and making love
Over the nasty sty!

(91–94)

This is the sex-disgust's crowning moment. "Seam" denotes animal grease. The sweats and juices of sex seep down into the "nasty sty" of the bed, stewing the honeying fornicators in their own corruption. Hamlet's "Go not to my uncle's bed" is the true successor to his impulsive "To a nunnery, go." Again he attempts by imperatives to create a woman who is not passion's slave. Again he wields the name of action in "go not." Again he reveals a counter-desire to defile the ideal he is fashioning:

> *Queen.*   What shall I do?
> *Hamlet.* Not this, by no means, that I bid you do:
> Let the bloat King tempt you again to bed,
> Pinch wanton on your cheek, call you his mouse,
> And let him, for a pair of reechy kisses,
> Or paddling in your neck with his damn'd fingers,
> Make you to ravel all this matter out
> That I essentially am not in madness,
> But mad in craft.
>
> (182–90)

Many critics have observed with L. C. Knights that Hamlet "is fascinated by what he condemns."[15] Critics who dislike psychoanalytic Shakespeare interpretation on the grounds of its supposed anachronism dwell on the absurdity of attributing unconscious conflicts to Renaissance characters. But how else can this speech be read? The switch into negation allows Hamlet to invert "go not" into "go," savoring the very sexual connection that disgusts him. Commands that would recreate chastity imaginatively bring back the whore.

After the closet scene Hamlet no longer rails against his mother and womankind in general. The question of whether he ever loved Ophelia has been left with the cruel drolleries of The Mousetrap. But the pattern holds good: his next declaration on the subject is positive. When the funeral procession arrives at the graveyard, and Hamlet is still in concealment, Laertes uses the word "fair" in direct reference to his sister's virginity: "Lay her 'i th' earth, / And from her fair and unpolluted flesh / May violets spring" (5.1.231–33). At just this point Hamlet recognizes the woman for whom the grave has been dug: "What, the fair Ophelia!" Once the mighty opposite of "honest," the word "fair" has lost its cargo of dishonesty. Jumping into Ophelia's grave to vie with Laertes for true ownership of the language of grief, Hamlet at last declares, "I lov'd Ophelia" (5.1.264).

But has he made an ally of Gertrude? She does not tell Claudius that Hamlet is mad in craft; the killing of Polonius was the deed of a man "mad as the sea and wind when both contend / Which is the mightier" (4.1.7–8), whose enfeebled brain really thought he was spearing a rat. Her aside on guilty apprehensiveness (4.5.17–20) proves that her conscience is still alert. When Gertrude sends word that Hamlet should "use some gentle entertainment to Laertes" before the fencing match (5.2.202–3), Hamlet appreciates her concern and moral authority: "She well instructs me" (204). At the match itself she is obviously his champion. Gertrude gives him a napkin to wipe his face, then carouses, fatally, to his unexpected success. Yet this is a matter decided in production. All a director need do is instruct his Gertrude to smile at Claudius, stand close to him, put her arm in his, and the audience will decide that Hamlet's attempt to sever them was simply ignored by a shallow and sensual queen.

In this regard the testimony of Q1 is suggestive. Although the many, often hilarious errors of the "bad quarto" are notorious, its most arresting novelty lies in fleshing out the alliance of Hamlet and Gertrude. It contains a short scene with no analogue in Q2 or F during which Horatio reveals to Gertrude that Hamlet has returned to Denmark. The queen repudiates her husband: "Then I perceive there's treason in his lookes / That seem'd to sugar o're his villanie."[16] Hamlet tells Gertrude in the closet scene that "when you are desirous to be blest, / I'll blessing beg of you" (172–73). Q1 brings the speech to fruition:

> *Queene.* Thankes be to heauen for blessing of the prince,
> Horatio once againe I take my leaue,
> With thowsand mothers blessings to my sonne.
>
> (1779–81)

I am not among the few who suppose Q1 to be either a garbled version of *Ur-Hamlet* or something like Shakespeare's rough draft, but I do believe that Q1's alliance between Gertrude and Hamlet reflects an early stage tradition.

The reconstitution of a family dispersed by villainy, misrecognition, and ill fortune is always the end-point in Shakespearean romance. To be sure, the peace at the end of Act 3 in *Hamlet* is an uncertain one dependent on the whims of production, and in any case temporary and insecure: the tragedy will end with the utter obliteration of the two main families of Denmark. But reference to romance's concluding renewals may indicate what Hamlet *has* achieved. He has rid his mind of any realistic motive for doubting the ghost, and can now act in "perfect conscience" (5.2.67). He is as free as he can hope to be from the mental infections of Gertrude's lust. In psychological terms the second and last appearance of King Hamlet to his son is wholly benign, defusing Hamlet's matricidal rage and directing him toward an empathic link with his mother. "Yes, you are a good son and have correctly separated my divinity from the devilishness of my unspeakable brother. But enough on that difference. Your real business just now is to renew your idealization of your mother. Speak to her, Hamlet, and without the daggers." When Hamlet does so, he for the first time obeys in concrete action an injunction of the ghost. And the ghost never appears again, as if it were in some manner already satisfied. We have the sense that, at least for the brief equilibrium at the end of Act 3, the king, queen, and prince have reason to feel that they have come to common ground, and retrieved their familial bonds, as much as may be, from the queen's remarriage.

The ledger has another side, however. Hamlet must answer for the murder of Polonius. Heaven will "punish me with this" (176): the bad dreams of damnation may just have come true. When he departs for England, his commanding stage presence temporarily deserting its kingdom, the play reveals the consequences on this earth in the death of Ophelia, the wrath of Laertes, and the alliance of Laertes and Claudius; the murder of Polonius comes back at Hamlet with deadly force. In the closet scene Hamlet concentrates whorishness in the royal bed of Denmark and tries to extricate his mother from the contamination. But the virgin/whore split cannot remain confined to Claudius's bed, for Hamlet has also forced its toxins on Ophelia. He loved her, he never loved her. She must go to a nunnery, she must be sexually explored in scathing witticisms. When Hamlet leaves the stage, the virgin/whore split dies away in the madness of Ophelia. We hear all about it in the old ballad she sings to tell us "what it means":

Pray let's have no more words of this, but when they ask you what it means, say you this.

[*sings*]

Tomorrow is Saint Valentine's day,
  All in the morning betime,
And I a maid at your window,
  To be your Valentine.
Then up he rose, and donn'd his clo'es,
  And dupp'd the chamber door,
Let in the maid that out a maid
  Never departed more.

By Gis and by Saint Charity,
  Alack and fie for shame,
Young men will do't if they come to't—
  By Cock, they are to blame.
Quoth she, "Before you tumbled me,
  You promis'd me to wed."

"So would I a done, by yonder sun,
And thou hadst not come to my bed."[17]
                          (4.5.48–55, 58–63, 65–66)

He will marry her if she gives him her virginity. He will not marry her because she gave him her virginity. Before a marriageable virgin, after an unmarriageable whore.[18] Hamlet and Ophelia have had no sexual connection, of course, but he has passed on to her the bitter paradoxes of male sexuality. The song speaks less to the history of Hamlet and Ophelia than to the psychic structures within which Hamlet rejected her. "Nymph, in thy orisons / Be all my sins remember'd." At the end of the rejection scene itself Ophelia ironically remembers Hamlet's greatness. "O, what a noble mind is here o'erthrown!" In her own overthrown mind she at last remembers the sins.

The plot line stemming from the death of Polonius will

lead to a grave, a curious prince, and a fateful funeral. Events in *Hamlet* being split, a second train of consequences also arises from that death. It is a plot line in the soul of the hero, enabling him to oppose a sea of troubles.

By my count Hamlet performs five rash acts in the play, and they reveal rashness to be a hit-or-miss affair. 1) Because his "fate cries out" (1.5.81), he ignores the advice of Horatio and Marcellus and follows the beckoning ghost of his father. It is impossible to place a negative judgment on the act that generates the drama. Moreover, his violent resistance to the advice of Horatio, threatening to kill anyone who seeks to restrain him, looks forward to his calmer and philosophical defiance of Horatio's advice in his fifth and final rash act. 2) He kills Polonius — a mistake. As Gertrude says, "O what a rash and bloody deed is this!" 3) On rash impulse he reads the documents Rosencrantz and Guildenstern bear to England, whereupon he forges new letters in a fair hand, seals them with his father's signet, and sends his meddlesome chums to an English death. This deed, a welcome show of aggression to all but the most moralistic critics, elicits his famous praise of rashness. 4) He jumps into the grave to grapple with Laertes, at which point the two plot lines stemming from the death of Polonius converge. Good for a well-made play, a disaster for the hero. For this fourth instance of rashness is cursed. It aids Claudius in transforming the cross-generational struggle between himself and Hamlet into a same-generational struggle between Laertes and Hamlet, symbolic brothers, and thus to pass down in time "the primal eldest curse" (3.3.37). 5) Defying augury, he goes to the fencing match. This last act is somewhat paradoxically a deliberate rashness, justified in serious theological terms. Like the first, the concluding rashness seems beyond the divisions of judgment, a mixture of good and evil fortune. Rashness gives (the uncovering of the English plot), rashness takes away (the murder of Polonius, the fight with Laertes), or both gives and takes away, as in following the ghost and submitting to the fencing game. Its report card runs from A to F to A/F, like the declarations of regard for Ophelia.

In some degree rashness may be viewed as the successor to Hamlet's vision of a world contaminated by his mother's lust. The second of the rash acts is obviously driven by the anger of the moment, which is primarily anger toward his mother; he scarcely bothers to acknowledge the deed, and launches into his tirade about the yawning gap between King Hamlet and King Claudius. At the end of the scene, anger stilled, he foretells his next rash act and its upshot:

> There's letters seal'd, and my two schoolfellows,
> Whom I will trust as I will adders fang'd—
> They bear the mandate, they must sweep my way
> And marshal me to knavery. Let it work;
> For 'tis the sport to have the enginer
> Hoist with his own petard.
>
> (3.4.204–9)

Hamlet's intuitions seem already to suspect the diplomatic pouch of his treacherous friends. All rashness need do is unseal "letters seal'd." Hamlet has gained a new confidence in his alliance with Gertrude. "Let it work": he need not have a plan; somehow he will foil his schoolfellows and the monarch they serve. A son is always at his best when his mother can appreciate "the sport." The new confidence and the old rage combine in impulsiveness. It is as if he has taught himself the imperative "go," the name of action hurled at both of the women in his life. For a man who would act both rashly and successfully, the readiness is all.

Those commands were intended to preserve or renew chastity. Considered as a mode of acting apart from its results, rashness also has about it a kind of purity:

> Rashly—
> And prais'd be rashness for it: let us know
> Our indiscretion sometime serves us well
> When our deep plots do pall.
>
> (5.2.6–9)

There is as usual a background contradiction, since the praise of rash action serves in the passage itself to delay the narration of a rash action. But I leave the stylistics of the nightmind to postmodernists. Hamlet's "let us know" indicates a decisive realization. The antic disposition has not been of much use. All deep plotting has done for Hamlet is prove to thought that the ghost was honest. It has changed nothing in the world. Thought poses questions, dividing action into mighty opposites. It looks before and after, reconstructing history to determine action's cause and scanning possible worlds to assess action's effect. It worries about satisfying standards. Will this be revenge enough? It accuses itself. It spends its time being appalled that it must "like a whore unpack my heart with words / And fall a-cursing like a very drab, / A scullion! Fie upon't! Foh!" Thought has determined that thought cannot, in respect for the deep consequences to thought, end itself. Rashness is the best substitute for suicide.

Rash acts, which never pass through thought, are unsullied by its hesitations and conflicts, ideals and disillusionments.[19] They circumvent the whorishness of angry and impotent words. When ready to go, they go. Like nuns and penitent adulteresses, they offer themselves for amendment to the deepest plotter of all:

> and that should learn us
> There's a divinity that shapes our ends,
> Rough-hew them how we will—
>
> (9–11)

Consequences are not in the end ours to reckon. If the results of rash action are split, it must be the will of God. In Act 5 deity becomes the main presence in the nightmind, replacing the faded ghost.

I have characterized Hamlet's respect for rashness as a kind of renewed mental virginity, but its association with his father suggests another current of idealization. Adelman argues that Hamlet identifies with his father and with God in the full psychoanalytic sense when using his father's signet: "Unexpectedly finding this sign of the father on his own person, Hamlet in effect registers his repossession of the idealized father within; and, like a good son, Hamlet can finally merge himself with this father, making His will his own."[20] It is certainly suggestive that Hamlet feels "heaven ordinant" (5.2.48), heaven ordaining, in having on his person his father's signet, though it is not to be forgotten that he uses this object to counterfeit the official will of Claudius. The signet so happily in his possession is "the model [replica] of that Danish seal," the one Claudius has used to seal his fate in England: identification with King Hamlet is as always contaminated with Claudius.

The prince does exude a general feeling of triumphant luckiness in his tale of rashness on the high seas. He has been stood in good stead! He can get away with murder!

Divine and earthly fathers seem to be cooperating; even the ability to write a fair hand, which Hamlet until now considered a "baseness," and "labor'd much / How to forget that learning" (5.2.34–35), proves the foresight of some unappreciated teacher. This sense of well-being, of having been unexpectedly provided by early authorities with the wherewithall necessary to reroute the lethal scheme of his opponent, stems from a confluence of identifications with a chaste mother and a provident father. Hamlet has within him, as active psychic agencies, the family that briefly reassembled during the closet scene. But there is something new as well—ordinant divinity, taught to us not by reason but by subrational happenstance, a lucky indiscretion—and the possibility of an alliance with his mysterious ways is the matter explored in the graveyard scene.

5 The Last Mystery

A s I finished this book, I was visited by a friend of pragmatic temperament. "Yes, I suppose so," he said on hearing of my admiration for the scene between Hamlet and the gravedigger. "But I don't have the slightest idea what it means." What defeats my pragmatic friend, I think, is that the graveyard scene offers nothing but meaning. With respect to the battle between Hamlet and Claudius, it accomplishes nothing. Hamlet does not form a plan. He does not happen on useful information. Shakespeare, grandly at his leisure, finds time to bring Hamlet and Horatio, eventually the entire Danish court and the mortal remains of Ophelia, to the local graveyard — only the second scene in the play (the first is 4.2, its locale unspecified) set outside Elsinore Castle. Two months or so before the play begins, Hamlet returned from Wittenberg to attend his father's funeral, which might have been held on this very ground.[1] "Foul deeds will rise, / Though all the earth o'erwhelm them, to men's eyes" (1.3.257–58). Hamlet is thinking of his father rising from the earth of his grave; when he first sees the ghost, he refers to it as a "dead corse" (1.4.52). Shakespeare reassembles his characters on the graveyard from which the foul deeds rose. It is where they are destined to go, and will go again when their dead bodies are heaped on a stage at the end of the play. The graveyard comes before the beginning, before the end, after the end. This scene does not advance the plot but stretches it out from dust to dust.

When I remarked in Chapter 2 that 3.4 was the greatest scene in *Hamlet,* I may have been rash. Planted in the design of the graveyard scene are specific messages for the prince, delivered one after another like tolling bells that summon to his remembrance things past, from his birth to his current embroilments. Like the closet scene, the graveyard scene stamps seals of fated specificity on Hamlet's life. But here the horizons are the largest imaginable. The scene casts the life of the hero, all the lives of all the characters, tragedy itself, in the broadest and most reductive perspective. It completes the ideal-making self-education of the prince, countering the wish that opens his first soliloquy with hard fact: instead of melting, thawing, and resolving into a dew, his flesh, all flesh, will leak into the waters, dusts, and dirts of mother earth. Here as elsewhere, the Shakespearean drama of splitting requires concepts that level and plot devices that reunite, such as the bed-tricks of *All's Well That Ends Well* and *Measure for Measure.* The graveyard scene in *Hamlet,* into which all its characters and motives and themes are funneled, envelops the play in a powerful spirit of counter-splitting. "For this whole world," as Donne observes, "is but an *universall church-yard,* but our *common grave*" (*Sermons* 10:234).

The peculiar structure of the revenge plot, in which a determining crime has taken place before the opening of the play, makes *Hamlet* itself seem like the conclusion of a tragedy already under way. In another structuring of the plot, closer to what we find in *The Murder of Gonzago,* Hamlet might be a character who appears in Act 4 of *The Hystorie of Claudius* to set the catastrophe in motion. He might appear even later in *The Tragicall Hystorie of King Hamblet and Queene Gertrude.* (Running parallel to *Hamlet* is a chronicle history, *Fortinbras of Norway,* in which the prince does not have a line.) Another way to describe this sense of a tragedy caught up in previous tragedies is "being under a curse." Claudius observes that his rank offense "hath the primal eldest curse upon't— / A brother's murder" (3.3.36–37). Cain is the first murderer, Abel the first corpse. Trying to wean Hamlet of excessive grief, Claudius takes him back to that very body:

> To reason most absurd, whose common theme
> Is death of fathers, and who still hath cried
> From the first corse till he that died today,
> "This must be so."

(1.2.103–4)

In the graveyard scene Shakespeare locates his tragedy in the same inclusive framework of "This must be so" that Claudius places grief. Significantly, it is not Abel who puts in an imaginative appearance, but Cain. There is a message for revengers in *Hamlet*'s graveyard.

It is obvious from the first that the gravedigger will make

an excellent conversational partner for Hamlet. No one else in the play has been up to it, and the prince has won victory after victory on the battlefields of wit. The fellow may suffer here and there from the dyslexia Shakespeare habitually imposes on the lower orders, but he likes riddles, speaks ironically, and respects a good foil: "I like thy wit well in good faith" (5.1.45). His conversation moves from the questionable ruling on Ophelia's death to privilege itself:

> *Gravedigger.*   And the more pity that great folk should have countenance in this world to drown or hang themselves more than their even-Christen. Come, my spade. There is no ancient gentlemen but gardeners, ditchers, and gravemakers—they hold up Adam's profession. [*He digs.*]
> *Other.* Was he a gentleman?
> *Gravedigger.* A was the first that ever bore arms.
> *Other.* Why, he had none.
> *Gravedigger.* What, art a heathen? How does thou understand the Scripture? The Scripture says Adam digged. Could he dig without arms? I'll put another question to thee. If thou answerest me not to the purpose, confess thyself—
>
> (27–39)

Like death, the sexton unmakes distinctions. The notion of "even-Christen" ought to abolish the exemptions given to "great folk." Adam bore arms, the sexton bears arms, and uses them as he speaks to dig Ophelia's grave. If Hamlet were around to hear him, he would receive a veiled message about the end of the play, where he will take arms against a sea of troubles in a sword fight. The piece of professional aggrandizement that makes Adam's tilling of the ground into the digging of graves serves as a grinning medieval introduction to Hamlet's forthcoming reflections. For the biblical digging has to do with agriculture, the food we fallen gentlemen labor in order to eat, whereas graves are made for corpses, the food we fallen gentlemen become. The transposition from farmer to gravemaker is of course appropriate inasmuch as Adam, the former gardener, made all our graves. The stage is set in large theological terms for Hamlet to encounter one last time the "rank unweeded garden" of his fallen world.

Arriving on the scene, Hamlet is first taken with the rough irreverence of the sexton. "Has this fellow no feeling of his business a sings in grave-making?" But his is not a dainty job. The language throughout this scene has a sharp concussive physicality: "Cudgel thy brains no more," "How the knave jowls it to th' ground," "chapless, knocked about the mazzard with a sexton's spade," "knock him about the sconce with a dirty shovel." A nineteenth-century edition is eloquent on the second of these examples: "If proof were wanted of the exquisite propriety and force of effect with which Shakespeare uses words, and words of even homely fashion, there could hardly be a more pointed instance than the verb 'jowls' here. What strength it gives to the impression of the head and cheek-bone smiting against the earth! and how it makes the imagination feel the bruise in sympathy!"[2] The speaker of these knockabout homely terms is Hamlet himself. He welcomes the impudent digging into his style.

A long parade of Adam's progeny must have come to this burial ground. To bury one is to displace another.[3] Out of the crowded earth a first skull is thrown up. Again Hamlet observes indignity, the low indifferent to the high:

> That skull had a tongue in it, and could sing once. How the knave jowls it to th' ground, as if 'twere Cain's jaw-bone, that did the first murder. This might be the pate of a fine politician which this ass now o'er-offices, one that would circumvent God, might it not? (74–79)

The rough treatment might be justified if it were the skull of Cain, Claudius's great original. Hamlet will imagine many identities for the skulls in this graveyard, but Cain is the first message he gets: fratricides come to this, their transgressions covered like all transgressions in the general sentence of mortality. The killing of a brother is *not* the primal eldest curse. What is history but God's curse on human sin? Savoring the way he intends to transform Rosencrantz and Guildenstern's plot against him into a plot against them, Hamlet remarks, "O, 'tis most sweet / When in one line two crafts directly meet" (3.4.211–12). Those who would circumvent God come always to this most sweet end, buried by God's plot in a plot of earth.

With the shift to the "fine politician," Hamlet's initial sense of social indignity yields to pleasure. Being rough with the high and mighty: there's a good game to be found in this, a "fine revolution and we had the trick to see't." One can imagine the skull to be that of a fawning courtier or a pompous lord, anyone deserving a comeuppance in the end. The roughness of the sexton passes into the rough justice of death. Though Hamlet is almost dazed throughout his graveyard lessons, like a child learning for the first time the facts of death, his initial distaste remains: "Did these bones

cost no more the breeding but to play at loggets with 'em?
Mine ache to think on't" (5.1.90–91). The simultaneous presence of entrancement and revulsion should remind us of his
earlier bouts of sex-disgust. As we will see, the substitution
of death for sex is one of the underlying tasks of this scene.

"I will speak to this fellow" (115). The man's close provincial wits make a job out of extracting simple information.
Hamlet is forced to occupy the role that the Danish court
has occupied with respect to him: "How absolute the knave
is. We must speak by the card or equivocation will undo us"
(133–34). This is like one of Polonius's asides when trying
to pump an antic Hamlet. The question "How long hast
thou been gravemaker?" throws up another message: "Of
all the days i' th' year I came to't that day that our last King
Hamlet o'ercame Fortinbras" (139–40). Then another message, this one with Hamlet's name on it: "It was that very
day that young Hamlet was born—he that is mad and sent
into England" (142–44). A career that began on the day of
his father's famous triumph, also the day of his own birth,
brings Hamlet into the presence of fate. This man may actually dig his grave; symbolically he has been digging it from
the day Hamlet was born. Hamlet asks his death-dealing
double about Hamlet,[4] "How came he mad?" (151). This is
the mystery that everyone at court (and perhaps Hamlet
himself) has been trying to solve. Like death, the sexton's
answer is rough and reductive:

> *Gravedigger.* Very strangely, they say.
> *Hamlet.* How "strangely"?
> *Gravedigger.* Faith, e'en with losing his wits.
> *Hamlet.* Upon what ground?
> *Gravedigger.* Why, here in Denmark.

> (151–55)

Everything that has preoccupied Hamlet—the adultery, murder, and incest, the injunctions of the ghost, the suicidal dilemma—is collected in the question "Upon what ground?" The play, the poetry, the great speeches, the thoughts: everything that makes Hamlet Hamlet and *Hamlet Hamlet* is collected in that question. What ground? "Why, here in Denmark," the sexton answers, that absolute knave. This is, I trust, the comic relief. Normally one thinks of comic relief as a boon to an overtaxed audience, but here the reduction of maddened wits to graveyard ground foretells an improvement in the spirits of the tragic hero.

As with the skull whose "fine pate" is "full of fine dirt," Hamlet's thought is turned into ground—Danish ground, the ground upon which he stands, the ground in which all his sufferings and all other sufferings will be buried. He seems to leap at this literalism, for his next question begins a long and strikingly concrete investigation into what happens to corpses in the ground. "How long will a man lie i' th' earth ere he rot?" Forced into repeated reflections on heaven and hell, the afterlife of the soul, he now meditates on the earthy afterlife of the body. *Hamlet*'s nightmind includes a groundmind or gravemind that is kinetic rather than inert. We do not rest in peace.

The first sign that Hamlet might be interested in the fate of dead bodies appears in the context of conception:

Hamlet. For if the sun breed maggots in a dead dog, being a good kissing carrion—Have you a daughter?
Polonius. I have, my lord.
Hamlet. Let her not walk i' th' sun. Conception is a blessing, but as your daughter may conceive—friend, look to't.

(2.2.181–86)

"What a prodigy it is," Montaigne exclaims, "that the drop of seed from which we are produced bears in itself the impressions not only of the bodily form but of the thoughts and inclinations of our fathers! Where does that drop of fluid lodge this infinite number of forms? And how do they convey these resemblances with so heedless and irregular a course that the great-grandson will correspond to his great-grandfather, the nephew to the uncle?"[5] What was this drop of infinite forms to Claudius's sex-disgusted nephew-son but sunlight (sonlight) infesting carrion with maggots? Yet Hamlet has outgrown those portraits of sullied marital blessings. When he lugs the guts of Polonius out of his mother's door, he pulls putrefaction out of conception. Dissolution, no longer a metaphor, is a thing in itself that behaves like a witty system of metaphors, creating unexpected fusions. In answer to the question of where Polonius is, Hamlet replies that he is "At supper, . . . Not where he eats, but where a is eaten" (4.3.17–20), and launches into reflections about how a king, become a worm, become a fish, might wind up in the guts of a beggar. Once obsessed with the facts of life, he is now fixated on the facts of death.

The graveyard scene begins with the posing of riddles. Who builds strongest? The gravemaker, since his houses last to doomsday (despite evictions!). The riddle points to death, certainly an abiding source of riddles. Is there life after death? What sort of life? The ghost of King Hamlet, leaving our riddles intact, is forbidden "to tell the secrets of my prison-house" (1.5.14). Contemplating the riddles of conception and birth, whose unfolding Freud thought inseparable from the achievement of a mature psyche, has brought Hamlet no enlightenment whatsoever, just rage, misogyny, and disillusionment;[6] but this scene effects his return to "something after death" (3.1.78), the riddles at the other end of life. As he did not in his meditations on conception and birth, Hamlet will find room for wisdom in his encounter with death — a truth he can live with, even embrace.

As he works, the gravedigger sings three stanzas of Lord Vaux's "The aged lover renounceth love," a poem in which the speaker bids farewell to the "lusty life" of youth and prepares himself for the grave:[7]

A pickaxe and a spade, a spade,
   For and a shrouding-sheet;
Oh a pit of clay for to be made
   For such a guest is meet.

                      (92–95)

Gascoigne notes that the poem "was thought by some to be made upon his death-bed" (Furness, 1:380). The singing gravedigger makes the "pit of clay" requested by the man in the song. More than he yet knows, Hamlet is that man. For the last message embedded in this fateful scene reveals the identity of the woman this grave will hold:

Hamlet. What, the fair Ophelia!
Gertrude. Sweets to the sweet. Farewell.
I hop'd thou shouldst have been my Hamlet's wife:
I thought thy bride-bed to have deck'd, sweet maid,
And not have strew'd thy grave.

                     (235–39)

It is the grave of Hamlet's irresolute youth, the marriage never to be. Like the speaker of Vaux's poem, Hamlet moves from first things to last things without the mature flowerings first things normally promise.

As once he stared at female faces, so now he stares at

skulls. What does he learn? The book and volume of a brain, once the seat of memory in the back, reason in the middle, commonsense and imagination in the front, becomes in the end a wad of ground or a hollow stench—truly a dirty mind. This is not the "easeful death" Keats was sometimes half in love with; Hamlet is falling in love with death as insult. One element of the scene's lesson is simple and nonsectarian, as old as the hills. Death, playing no favorites, delivers the supreme rebuke to human pride. "You know, what busie path so ere you tread / To greatnesse, you must sleep among the dead."[8] No matter how great one is, how powerful, how ambitious, he will lie down in darkness and have his light in ashes. High and low, man and woman, prince and pauper, jester and king: death undoes all the terms that divide and separate human beings by reducing difference to indistinction.[9]

There is a second part to the lesson. It has to do with literal dissolution, death's attack on the integrity of the body. Donne writes of "*death* after *death*," imitating his subject in expansive renamings: "But for us that dye now and sleepe in the state of the dead, we must al passe this *posthume* death, this *death* after *death,* nay this death after buriall, this *dissolution* after *dissolution,* this death of *corruption* and *putrifaction,* of *vermiculation* and *incineration,* of *dissolution* and *dispersion* in and *from* the grave" (*Sermons* 10:238). The moral specific to this death after death begins to take root in the vividness of Hamlet's descriptions of the gravedigger. It is closer to consciousness in his identification of the skulls with vain and pompous men now given to "Lady Worm" (87). It almost surfaces in his address to Yorick's skull.

We have come at last to Yorick, the best-known skull in

the graveyard, who for some reason has occasioned more sentimentality in the history of *Hamlet* criticism than any other figure in the play. He was a fine fellow, and full of infinite jest. But the critics dwell intolerably on his fineness. "Repulsed by death, Hamlet remembers Yorick as someone once wonderfully alive, his tongue the instrument of jests, his throat the instrument of song, his wit the stimulus of other men's laughter. Life is valuable in itself. It is better to be, or to have been, if like Yorick one can be fully human, not earth-contaminated like the politician, the courtier, and the lawyer."[10] To which I say, pah! Is he so fine as to revise "To be or not to be" and banish from the end of the play Hamlet's low estimate of the world? In psychoanalytic criticism Yorick is the good father, unearthed at last to provide an alternative to the legendary father and the contemptible stepfather:

> Here I want to add a third aspect of the father that is most subtly introduced. I believe that Yorick is a thinly disguised father image. He is the tenderly loving, affectionate father, with "those lips that I have kissed I know not how oft," who "hath borne me on his back a thousand times." He is the only person in the entire play of whom Hamlet speaks with unreserved tenderness. He died when Hamlet was seven—which suggests when the repression of that relationship occurred. It had indeed been a fateful relationship: Hamlet had thereafter become a great jester, too. The identification with Yorick seems to have been quite strong. Hamlet's feminine passive relationship to his father is of course the most dangerous of all, and he remembers it only in connection with a substitute figure and within the context of death.[11]

The author is a psychoanalyst, not a literary critic, and I do not begrudge him his crude biographical imagining any more than I would Bradley's. That Hamlet remembers Yorick as a performer, a successful jester who kept the table roaring, suggests some form of identification. No doubt this "whoreson mad fellow" (170) contributed some stylistic flourishes to Hamlet's antic disposition. Shakespeare was interested in fools at this point in his career—Touchstone in *As You Like It* (such a fascination to Jaques), Feste in *Twelfth Night,* Parolles at the end of *All's Well.* None of these are jesters to a king; a resurrected Yorick will one day be given a plum role in *King Lear.* His services are not required in *Hamlet* because the prince in his variety is himself a fool, using the fool's techniques of riddle, literalism, and apparent lunacy to draw the court into booby-trapped mazes of infinite antic jest. But just now in *Hamlet* the main business is neither a salute to foolery nor a last minute revelation of a good alternative father.

Passages like the two I have quoted are found throughout the field. Almost everyone cuddles up to Yorick. Maybe the critics sense that Hamlet is creating an ideal, and therefore sponsor his efforts with exaggerations of their own, beholding "unreserved tenderness" and a "feminine passive" demeanor. The text itself is wilder and more interesting. Hamlet is in fact discovering an ideal, but the ideal is not Yorick:

> *Hamlet.*   Alas, poor Yorick. I knew him, Horatio, a fellow of infinite jest, of most excellent fancy. He hath borne me on his back a thousand times, and now—how abhorred in my imagination it is. My gorge rises at it. Here hung those lips that I have kissed I know

not how oft. Where be your gibes now, your gambols, your songs, your flashes of merriment, that were wont to set the table on a roar? Not one now to mock your own grinning? Quite chop-fallen? Now get you to my lady's chamber and tell her, let her paint an inch thick, to this favour she must come. Make her laugh at that—Prithee, Horatio, tell me one thing.

Horatio. What's that, my lord?

Hamlet. Dost thou think Alexander looked o' this fashion i' th' earth?

Horatio. E'en so.

Hamlet. And smelt so? Pah! [*Puts down the skull.*]

(178–94)

The imagination of Yorick alive becomes "now," in the presence of Yorick's skull, an abhorrence. That is why Hamlet stresses the affectionate character of his memory of the jester: he is alive to the contrast, his disgust as sharp as his memories are tender. At the thought that he has kissed the lips without any apprehension of the skull beneath, his "gorge rises."

Unwilling to remain a captive to revulsion, a violent Hamlet has labored to make ideals out of sex-disgust. The new death-disgust also passes into aggression. Death has taunted and humiliated Yorick, and Hamlet takes the part of death, staging a triumph of mockery. "Not one now to mock your own grinning?" The last joke is on the jester. Yorick, victim of death's zingers, has no more comic inventions. Hamlet gloats over his melancholy silence. "Quite chop-fallen?" He discovers a satisfying use for the black humor of death: "get you to my lady's chamber." As painting to the face, so the face to the skull. In grave graves hyprocrisy gets stripped away, leaving a skeletal core that smiles and smiles and still seems disgusting. Death after death, not Yorick, is the ideal being born in Hamlet's teeming brain.

Clearly struck by a thought, he wonders if Alexander, conqueror of the world, came to this end. Of course he did: death is not a splitter. But I think the submerged idea in the transition from Yorick to Alexander is that death, the death he has just verbally imitated, rough taunting death, is one hell of a revenger:

> *Hamlet.* To what base uses we may return, Horatio! Why, may not imagination trace the noble dust of Alexander till a find it stopping a bunghole?
> *Horatio.* 'Twere to consider too curiously to consider so.
> *Hamlet.* No, faith, not a jot, but to follow him thither with modesty enough, and likelihood to lead it. Alexander died, Alexander was buried, Alexander returneth to dust, the dust is earth, of earth we make loam, and why of that loam whereto he was converted might they not stop a beer-barrel?
>   Imperious Caesar, dead and turn'd to clay,
>   Might stop a hole to keep the wind away.
>   O that that earth which kept the world in awe
>   Should patch a wall t' expel the winter's flaw.
>   But soft, but soft awhile. Here comes the King,
>   The Queen, the courtiers.
>
> (196–211)

The tame Horatio uncharacteristically pulls back from the suggestion, perhaps because he senses the passionate aggression in Hamlet's death-tracing imagination. Again, this is not Romantic death, a pantheistic reunion with nature, the voluptuous death of Walt Whitman's endlessly rocking cradle. According to Donne, death after death "is the most inglorious and contemptible *vilification,* the most deadly and peremptory *nullification* of man, that wee can consider" (*Sermons* 10:239).[12] No ordinary considerer, Hamlet warms to the most nullifying of all man's thoughts of man, and insists on exploring the bunghole hypothesis through every stage of the transformation.[13] If a demonstration of the possibility of Alexander stopping a bunghole were the only thing at issue, the expansion of the idea to Caesar would be superfluous. Hamlet not only takes up the case of imperious Caesar, but also shifts to verse, clearly proud of his thought.

Hamlet has been flummoxed throughout his musings on revenge in part because he holds himself to a Senecan standard. He must drink hot blood, entertain bloody thoughts only. His sword must deliver a horrible hent, sending Claudius headlong to hell. Revenge is after all an art. The genre demands an escalation of horror, the vengeance exceeding the crime: *scelera non ulcisceris,/nisi uincis,* you do not avenge a crime unless you surpass it.[14] What Hamlet learns from tracing the corpses of the great empire-builders of the ancient world is that death always takes care of that excess. There is outrage enough in death for the case of Cain himself. He has imagined several "base uses" to which we may return; surely there are thousands more. Nature, inspired by God's curse, stops at nothing. A piece of Shakespeare might be lodged in the paper on which this book is printed, or in the stuffing of the chair on which I sit.[15] Stopping a bunghole or filling a crack in the wall: these are every bit as good as what Mortimer had done to Edward II, or Richard to his brother Clarence. The lessons of the graveyard scene relieve the pressures on Hamlet. Mothers at the beginning of life do not sully the flesh as profoundly as God at the end of life. Hamlet will avenge his father but need not plan a *bella vendetta* or a rivalrous Senecan atrocity. The task of revenge converts, as it were, to Christianity.[16] God's curse will handle the really rough stuff.

This is the great trick at the end of the play. Because Hamlet does not plan his revenge, he seems to have sacrificed some portion of his will. Conventional revengers are ambitious. They want to appall the gods, horrify the heavens. They want to be remembered for their artful horrors, achieving preeminence in the memorials of pay-back. The inner danger of the genre has always been that its heroes can become vindictive villains. As if to confirm that judgment, Kyd's Hieronomo bites out his tongue and commits suicide after achieving his revenge. Others take care to Christianize their tasks; Hamlet is not alone among patient revengers.[17] The genre demands of the revenger some trade-off between morality and self-respect. But it is the distinction of *Hamlet,* in the lesson that seizes the hero's mind when contemplating poor Yorick, to show that the moral path, abjuring Senecan plans and ends, can also satisfy the aggressions of the revenger. Christianity is made to seem fully compatible with Hamlet's vengeful spirit.

The trick does not work for everyone.[18] The history of *Hamlet* criticism shows the stubborn persistence of the linked ideas that revenge is evil and the ghost a demon. But the graveyard identification with death confuses the polarities of honorable vengeance and Christian morality. Death is our appointed end. To death we must finally submit. The devotional literature of the Renaissance is full of meditations on skulls or the indignities of the grave meant to

detach the self from worldly ties.[19] Finding an accomplice
in death, Hamlet has chosen the route of relative piety for
a life co-opted by this genre. Whatever he imagines to be in
store for Claudius is equally in store for him: there is no
splitting in death after death, and the revenger will get the
same rough treatment as his victim. Still, by locating his
vengeful passion in death's devastating severity Hamlet has
given the curse of mortality a keen classical edge.

He wins for himself the calm of 5.2. It is not quite the mysterious indifference envisioned by Harold Bloom. Rosencrantz and Guildenstern "are not near my conscience," but
Laertes is: "I am very sorry, good Horatio, / That to Laertes
I forgot myself" (75–76). He apologizes at length, if somewhat vaguely, before the fencing match. He takes care to
assess one final time the fit between his conscience and his
task:

> is't not perfect conscience
> To quit him with this arm? And is't not to be damn'd
> To let this canker of our nature come
> In further evil?
>
> (5.2.67–70)

Perfect conscience to do it, damnation not to do it. He is
not indifferent to damnation. He seems rather to have lost
his fear of it.

In this final scene Hamlet is no longer a seeker and
maker of ideals, but himself an ideal—a noble spirit fash-
ioned by himself with very little help from his world or his
genre. He has resigned himself to his presence in a hack-
neyed if still popular genre. Finally. Problems have become
strengths. Suicide and virginity combine in the readiness to
be rash, leaving the ends to God. The anger has been de-

tached from womanhood and turned solely toward Claudius. Taught that mortality will serve its interests, anger bides its time. An alliance with death has given melancholy, his old distraction, a new purpose. It won't be long now. Soon the news will arrive from England: "The interim is mine" (73).

After Osric departs, he is struck by a premonition concerning the match. But Hamlet is now beyond the timidities of prudent forethought. He need simply wait, holding the "something dangerous" (5.1.255) in him at the ready:

Horatio. You will lose, my lord.
Hamlet. I do not think so. Since he went into France, I have been in continual practice. I shall win at the odds. Thou wouldst not think how ill all's here about my heart; but it is no matter.
Horatio. Nay, good my lord.
Hamlet. It is but foolery, but it is such a kind of gaingiving as would perhaps trouble a woman.
Horatio. If your mind dislike anything, obey it. I will forestall their repair hither and say you are not fit.
Hamlet. Not a whit. We defy augury. There is special providence in the fall of a sparrow. If it be now, 'tis not to come; if it be not to come, it will be now; if it be not now, yet it will come. The readiness is all. Since no man, of aught he leaves, knows aught, what is't to leave betimes? Let be.

(5.2.205–20)

And the court, cushions, foils and daggers come forth, followed by the wine. The continual practice will be a help; heaven was ordinant in that. But even now, after the long journey from "A little more than kin, and less than kind" to

"I shall win at the odds," there is still a reason not to act, a crossroads to ponder.

To go or not to go, that is the question. Is the illness in his heart something to trouble over or something to defy? The moment can certainly be second-guessed, since his intuition correctly warns of danger. A thorough meditation might even consider that fact. "What if I ignore the premonition, go to the match, then later am sorry? In vain the will seeks alteration in the finished records of memory. O condition of the mind . . ." Finding one last use for the remnants of his misogyny, Hamlet dismisses as womanish the premonition and its demand to be unpacked in words by thinking over the problem of going or not going. He must rededicate himself to rashness. Horatio bathes him in a mother's concern. "If your mind dislike anything, obey it." He will tell the court Hamlet is not fit. "Not a whit," Hamlet replies, the crack of the rhyme slapping the idea's face.

"We defy augury." This evokes the egotistical sublime of Seneca, but has its true magnificence in being smaller and less desperate. Is the "we" royal? Does it denote the team of Hamlet and Horatio (and maybe Gertrude)? "We" might even include God: "There is special providence in the fall of a sparrow." Birds figured prominently in Roman augury, and Hamlet's reference to the gospel sparrow seems designed to call attention to the pointlessness of augury in a Christian dispensation, where fate has become providence.[20] The biblical context speaks to the folly of fearing those who may take your life: "and feare ye not them which kil the bodie, but are not able to kil the soule: but rather feare him, which is able to destroy soule and bodie in hel. Are not two sparrowes sold for a farthing, and one of them shall not fall on the ground without your Father? Yea, and all the heeres of your heade are nombred. Feare ye not therefore, ye are of more value than manie sparrows" (Matt. 10.28–31 Geneva). Only God should be feared, and that fear tempered by our knowledge of his love.

Augury tried to see ahead. Providence, God's business, means seeing ahead. Calvin, splitting providence, believed that his overseeing is not merely "general," the result of regularities set in motion at the creation of the world, but also "special," "whence it follows that providence is lodged in the act."[21] Special providence impresses itself on the situation, the moment, the particular sparrow. Every hair on one's head is numbered: we could not be told in plainer terms that God is an individualist. The prince of individualism is not as plotless as he may appear. At the end of the closet scene he declared himself an artful counterplotter, able to turn the ploys of Claudius to his own ends. He will do just that in the forthcoming fencing match. But through the concept of "special providence," a rare instance of Shakespeare's appeal to a specific and sectarian theological idea, Hamlet aligns his countering will with the supreme author of history's plot—which is to say, the plot of death, the counterplot to human crime. Into the hands of the divine craftmaster our plans are delivered, there to be shaped and fitted. The belief in special or singular providence, maintained Calvin (a careful student of Seneca), rids the mind of disquiet: "Gratitude of mind for the favorable outcome of things, patience in adversity, and also incredible freedom from worry about the future all necessarily follow upon this knowledge" (209). Shedding baggage, Hamlet leaves to God the task of looking out for himself.

He then utters three perfectly fateful sentences. Whatever

"it" means, "it" must happen either now or in the future. The statements are a trap for necessity, capturing fate. It is impossible that "it" be not now and be not to come. The very model for something that is sure to be either now or to come, that has to be one or the other, is death. But most readers and audiences take "it" to mean the occasion to kill Claudius as well. Claudius's chance at him, his chance at Claudius: these are the same thing now. The mighty opposites are trapped in the same graveyard sentences. We have in the double "it" (my death, his death) one last assertion of the doubling of the two characters. Moreover, Christianity comes into alliance with the revenge motive. Working in accord with rash action, providence in Act 5 absorbs death (it *will* come) and revenge (*it* will come). Hamlet assumes that he has earned the special providence, uniquely his own, of not dying without the opportunity for vengeance. His individuality, the main subject of his students from the Romantics on, has resolved the split in the genre between morality and satisfaction.

Remembering "To be or not to be," critics discern maturation in "Let be." Hamlet is now beyond the dilemma of wishing to escape his fate. Rather than trying to outthink God, he works with God, his fellow counterplotter. Insofar as he is still suicidal, heedlessly defying augury, the impulse to self-destruction has made a home for itself within the imperative to revenge. Jenkins will have none of this: "Many editors wrongly take this ['Let be'] to be part of Hamlet's reflections, expressing his resignation to the course of events. A misplaced ingenuity has even tried to make it answer 'To be or not to be.' But it merely recognizes an interruption which requires their dialogue to break off" (407). He is surely right that the immediate sense of "Let

be" is "No more time for this" rather than "Let the question of when death will come cease to distract us, since the
readiness is all," though I do not see why these two senses
are necessarily disjunctive. I also grant that it would take
an unrealistically attentive audience to hear in "Let be" an
echo of the famous soliloquy, though it counts toward the
meaningfulness of "Let be" that Hamlet echoes the phrase
("O, I could tell you — / But let it be" [5.2.342–43]) after receiving his death. Yet the evidence of the *Sonnets* proves
that Shakespeare was capable of writing in a manner that
wastes no opportunity for sense, and the smallest details of
his plays, rigorously interpreted by generations of critics,
keep falling into happy patterns. Hamlet says "Let be" as
the court materializes — his special providence, it. There is
no more time to talk out his justification for going to the
fencing match. The event is at hand; he is ready; let thoughts
be. Hamlet's consignment of a thoughtful moment to oblivion with "Let be" does seem in its way an answer to "To be
or not to be." He is no longer stymied by the conflicts of
internal argument. The pale cast of thought recovers the native hue of resolution.

We may now pause to consider the divinity that preoccupies our hero in the final act. Many have found it a barren
and etiolated Christianity, hardly distinguishable from the
stoic love of fate. They are surely right that it lacks the full-
ness and cultural ambition of the Christianity one asso-
ciates with Augustine, Aquinas, Luther, and Calvin, though
as we have seen it borrows from Calvin a special notion of
providence. Hamlet's narrowed faith has no concept of the
soul, no set of virtues and vices, no answer to the general
problems of mankind, no liturgy, no commandments, and
no Christ. I would argue that if the Hamlet of Act 5 *did* pro-

fess an expansive Christianity, we would find ourselves either out of revenge tragedy altogether, with a hero who turns against his appointed task and rejects his father's ghost, or stuck in a morally repellent revenge tragedy, with a hero whose continued dedication to vengeance would render his religiosity pointless. Hamlet's shaping and ordaining God is the theological construct of a specific man in a specific circumstance — a revenger in a revenge tragedy who must pursue "howsomever" (1.5.84) the death of Claudius, taint not his mind, leave his mother to heaven, and "remember" his father's ghost. His divinity can only be understood in the context of his individuality.

God cleans out and empties Hamlet's wild mind. "The time is out of joint," the prince declared after swearing Horatio and Marcellus to secrecy: "O cursed spite, / That ever I was born to set it right" (1.5.196–97). But God must shape rough ends, fitting together what is "out of joint." Hamlet need not produce a horrid vengeance to balance off his father's murder. He is not so much "born" to set it right — and here one must recall yet again the ugly thoughts that whirl about birth — as he must die to set it right. By identifying with death as pure annihilation, Hamlet escapes from his family-confined thoughts of birth and incest to claim a place in the entire history of mankind, whose microcosm is the crowded graveyard of 5.1. This is not all of death, as Horatio will remind us at the exact moment of Hamlet's passing. But death as loss and dissolution, consignment to the impersonal energies of matter, is exactly the aspect of death a revenger is capable of divinizing — a curse of utter humiliation. Such death is the core of tragedy, and in this respect Hamlet makes his very own the darkness of his genre.

To this death he adds "special providence," which I inter-

pret to mean a death uniquely his, and one that will not pre-
clude the killing of Claudius. When the ghost appears a
second time, he in effect asks Hamlet to see his mother dif-
ferently, as a suffering creature in need of wise counsel
rather than a contaminating enemy to be stabbed with
words. This act of moral imagination marks a shift from
birth, anger, self-sickening thought, and Senecan plotting
to death, calm, rash action, and special providence. After
pointing in this direction, toward the future, King Hamlet
recedes into the night, clearing room for God. The old command to avenge Claudius then rewrites itself in the language of divinity: what was initially Hamlet's promise to
obey the ghost and kill Claudius becomes God's promise
that Hamlet will indeed obey the ghost and kill Claudius.
While I see the ghost's remains in the God of the final act,
I am reluctant to call this God a refiguration of the father,
the mother, or the still earlier "combined parent concept"
that Ernest Jones detected in the play.[22] My psychoanalytic
instincts tell me that the human mind conserves and refash-
ions, stringing out origins in complex ends; yet my instincts
as a student of *Hamlet* tell me that it would be wrong, completely wrong, to pull the hero back into the confinement of
his beginnings. All of the ghost's commands will be obeyed,
save the last. In Act 5 the ghost is gone and unremembered.
King Hamlet and Queen Gertrude, insofar as they represent the fountainheads of his mental distress, are forgotten
in God. In his detailed probing of "death after death" Hamlet learns both the universal sovereignty of his aggression
and the secret of peacefulness. His peacefulness is that of
someone given a terrible peremptory task, so peremptory
that "I do not know / Why yet I live to say this thing's to
do" (4.4.43–44), who gradually realizes that his task is

nothing less than the everyday business of the gravedigging God of this world. Sooner or later, it will come.

If ever a scene illustrated that a divinity shapes our ends, rough-hew them as we may, it is the end of *Hamlet*. Claudius was right in supposing that a blasé Hamlet would not bother to peruse the foils (4.7.132–35). The three traps laid for the hero—unbuttoned sword, envenomed sword, the cup of poisoned wine—are nonetheless turned around against their makers, though not until Hamlet's death is already in him. First the tip of the blade and its poison: "The point envenom'd too! Then, venom, to thy work." But one must be sure at a time like this. And it is not vengeance enough to puncture Claudius at sword's length. Hamlet wants to get into his face. Cup in hand, he moves to the kill:[23]

> Here, thou incestuous, murd'rous, damned Dane,
> Drink off this potion. Is thy union here?
> Follow my mother.
>
> (5.2.230–32)

The drunken king whose loud carouses Hamlet excoriated on the way to meet the ghost, the poisoner who smiles and smiles and can still be a villain: death at the smile, death in a drink, death in the metaphor of revelry, death through the jawbones, is fitted to both his crime and his concealment of it. Bradley heard the venom and wit in "union." Hamlet kills the marriage in ironically affirming the marriage.[24] If "union" means "marriage" as well as "pearl," it must also allude to the sexual union marriage celebrates.[25] "Follow my mother": go to my mother's bed, uncle. As we follow this poisonous jest's lines of filiation back through the play, leading us to the sources of Hamlet's anguish, we realize that this is exactly what he would say, and must say. He has held in readiness for this climactic occasion his old ambivalent hatred for the sexual bond between Gertrude and Claudius. His special providence is to have won from grief, doubt, and disillusionment this moment of consummate contempt.

He holds on to the cup. Horatio tries to seize it from him, but Hamlet wrests it from his grasp: "As th'art a man, / Give me the cup. Let go, by Heaven I'll ha't." Only Gertrude and Claudius are to drink from the cup. It is their union. Horatio must "Let go": again the imperative of action descended from "Get thee to a nunnery" and "To a nunnery, go." The impulse throughout has been to save someone. He could not rescue Ophelia from the wounds he inflicted on her life. He could not rescue Gertrude from the fate of Claudius. His apology was too little and too late to help Laertes. But he does save Horatio, supplying the only reason that could possibly dissuade his friend from following him. Horatio must do him the favor of ministering to his "wounded name." If no one knows aught of aught they leave, what is it to leave betimes? Such indifference is ultimately too severe. He cannot leave a vilified name, for this revenger has fought with outstanding courage to make ideals and become an ideal. When the story is told, full of unnatural acts and purposes mistook, he will not be remembered for his revenge, though it is memorable enough and fulfills the genre's expectations. But he has not competed in horrors.

The sergeant of the gravemind, home to everything but the soul, arrests thought. "Good night, sweet prince": Hamlet splits in half, a body no longer alive, a soul we can no longer know; base remains for the long benighted "feast" (5.2.370) of death, sweet untainted spirit (so we hope) for the everlasting day of eternal rest. The kingdom is passed on. Arrangements are made. Like Gertrude at the grave of Ophelia, Fortinbras remembers the promise that is not to be: "For he was likely, had he been put on, / To have prov'd most royal." Guns discharge their sound and fury, signifying "the soldier's music and the rite of war" — signifying nothing with respect to Hamlet, whose honor was of a different order. We have been privy to his inner counsels and deepest plots, the intimate revelations of his seven soul-baring soliloquies. We know one thing he never knows — the hindsight that Claudius might have been killed and damned as he knelt in the chapel. In cases where we have been allowed to see ahead (that Polonius is concealed behind the arras, that the trip to England is a death plot, that the grave being dug is for Ophelia, that the fencing match is a death plot), Hamlet has eventually caught up with us, purging dramatic irony from our spectatorship. The audience's sense of the meaning of the play has been the meaning he gave it. But now we are alone, and to avert the collapse of meaning our minds reach toward him. Hamlet at last becomes what he fought to escape: thoughts. As the guns reverberate we probably remember in a confused way his words and deeds, our long fascination with the role now ended. It is not a minor task of *Hamlet* criticism to give shape to those inchoate recollections.

I cannot say good night to him without remembering the moment at which the command of vengeance was first a mental fact:

> Hold, hold, my heart,
> And you, my sinews, grow not instant old,
> But bear me stiffly up. Remember thee?

Ay, poor ghost, whiles memory holds a seat
In this distracted globe. Remember thee?
Yea, from the table of my memory
I'll wipe away all trivial fond records,
All saws of books, all forms, all pressures past
That youth and observation copied there,
And thy commandment all alone shall live
Within the book and volume of my brain,
Unmix'd with baser matter. Yes, by heaven!
O most pernicious woman!
O villain, villain, smiling damnèd villain!

(1.5.93–106)

Had Hamlet been able to limit himself to one untrammeled thought, "Thou shalt avenge," we would pair him with Titus Andronicus, who writes vows of vengeance in his study and rises to greet Tamora in the guise of Revenge (*Tit* 5.2). But Hamlet's first vision of his perfection is not to be his last. Already the baser matter of *mater* intrudes in "most pernicious woman," trailing with her the forms and pressures of youth.[26] Vengeance must share this mind with clamoring disillusionment: such is the tragic hand dealt to the forger of modern consciousness. Maturity of the ordinary sort is out of the question—no degree from Wittenberg, no marriage, no reign, no memorable military exploit. He can excel only in the way he leaves his mother to heaven, takes vengeance on Claudius, and arrives at his own death with an unsullied mind. It is evident from the beginning that if Hamlet is to succeed as a revenger, he must succeed as a thinker of contaminated thoughts, finding strategies of cooperation for a divided consciousness. Baser matter, as it turns out, whether in thoughts or in bodies, mixes with everything. His horror of mixture, of splits collapsed, must come to terms with—must seek its peace in—the great grim mixture of death. He does exactly that, and from a spoiled heritage generates his extraordinary composure of soul in the final act.

How different his last idea of revenge is from his first! What a false ideal this seems from the perspective of the end! The first paternal visit is disastrous; the second shows the way to the poise of Act 5. Virtually everything in *Hamlet*, down to the finest details of writing and plotting, is divided and yet paired. Granted, the impression of transformation in the last act rests on two speeches only, the praise of rashness and the defiance of augury. Yet these speeches have behind them the theological sweep and psychological authority of the graveyard scene: there we touch the base matter at the ground of his providential felicity.

We remember Hamlet for the effects of vengeance on his mind (Acts 1–4) and at last for his mind's effects on vengeance (Act 5). No Shakespearean character comes a longer way. Because he rewrote the book on revenge within the volume of his brain, he has been distracting our globes for two centuries.

Notes

Preface

1. Quoted in James M. Gibson, *The Philadelphia Shakespeare Story: Horace Howard Furness and the New Variorum Shakespeare* (New York: AMS, 1990), p. 220.

CHAPTER 1. *Hamlet* in History

1. The critical works discussed in this paragraph are, in order, Terence Hawkes, "*Telmah*," in *Shakespeare and the Question of Theory*, ed. Patricia Parker and Geoffrey Hartman (New York: Methuen, 1985), pp. 310–32; Marjorie Garber, *Shakespeare's Ghost Writers: Literature as Uncanny Causality* (New York: Methuen, 1987); David Leverenz, "The Woman in Hamlet: An Interpersonal View," in *Representing Shakespeare: New Psychoanalytic Essays,* ed. Murray M. Schwartz and Coppélia Kahn (Baltimore: Johns Hopkins Univ. Press, 1980), pp. 110–28; Annabel Patterson, *Shakespeare and the Popular Voice* (Cambridge, Mass.: Basil Blackwell, 1989).

2. Gary Taylor, *Reinventing Shakespeare: A Cultural History from the Restoration to the Present* (New York: Weidenfeld & Nicolson, 1989).

3. Paul Conklin's *History* (New York: King's Crown Press, 1947) does

treat the influence of theatrical production. A. A. Raven's *Hamlet Bibli-ography and Reference Guide, 1877–1935* (New York: Russell & Russell, 1966) is particularly useful in cataloguing and summarizing the great mass of *Hamlet* criticism in German. There are several books, such as John Jump, ed., *Shakespeare: Hamlet, A Casebook* (London: Macmillan, 1968), containing extracts from the prominent critics. Paul Gott-schalk's excellent *The Meanings of Hamlet* (Albuquerque: Univ. of New Mexico Press, 1972) divides the history of *Hamlet* criticism into schools. In his conclusion he glances at a future of "addition and consolidation" (p. 141). Writing two decades later, I cannot allow myself this confidence.

4. In Goethe's novel, the characters are rehearsing Shakespeare's trag-edy. Conklin, pp. 104–9, relates the book to the "Hamlet fever" in Ger-many in the late 1770s. See also the materials gathered in *Shakespeare in Germany, 1740–1815,* ed. R. Pascal (Cambridge: Cambridge Univ. Press, 1937).

5. *Hamlet* 1.5.96–97. All quotations are from the New Arden edition by Harold Jenkins (London: Methuen, 1981). Quotations from other plays also use the New Arden editions.

6. Barbara Everett, *Young Hamlet: Essays on Shakespeare's Tragedies* (Oxford: Clarendon Press, 1989), pp. 11–34. This view is also implicit in much of the psychoanalytic criticism of the play.

7. August Wilhelm Schlegel, *A Course of Lectures on Dramatic Art and Literature,* trans. John Black (London: Bohn, 1846), p. 404. For a late example of this interpretation, see Harry Levin, *The Question of Hamlet* (Oxford: Oxford Univ. Press, 1959), p. 85 ff.

8. Susanne Türck, *Shakespeare und Montaigne. Ein Beitrag zur Ham-let-Frage* (Berlin, 1930). Here I rely on Raven, *Hamlet Bibliography,* p. 93. "There is nothing either good or bad but thinking makes it so" echoes the title of Montaigne's essay "That the taste of good and evil depends in large part on the opinion we have of them" (*The Complete Essays of Mon-taigne,* trans. Donald M. Frame [Stanford: Stanford Univ. Press, 1965], pp. 33–46).

9. A. P. Rossiter discusses skepticism often in *Angel with Horns,* ed. Graham Storey (London: Longmans, 1961), especially in the great essay on *Troilus and Cressida;* Graham Bradshaw, in *Shakespeare's Skepticism* (Ithaca: Cornell Univ. Press, 1987), declares *Angel with Horns* "the most illuminating critical book on Shakespeare to be published in the period separating Bradley's *Shakespearean Tragedy* and Norman Rabkin's *Shake-speare and the Problem of Meaning*" (p. xii).

10. For the relationship between *roman* and "romantic" in Schlegel see Hans Eicher, *Friedrich Schlegel* (New York: Twayne, 1970), pp. 150–51. F. Schlegel's main discussion of *Hamlet* occurs in *Die Griechen und die Röman* of 1797.

11. Rossiter's chapter in *Angel with Horns* provides a good modern reading of the play closely in tune with the Romantics.

12. Thomas Middleton Raysor, ed., *Coleridge's Shakespeare Criticism*, 2 vols. (London: Constable, 1930), 1:54. Coleridge's vow of originality appears in 1:18–19. R. A. Foakes, a more recent editor, believes that he has established a chronology for the Coleridge lecture notes that confirms "Coleridge's general claim that he reached the basic positions exemplified in Schlegel's account of Shakespeare independently and before he had read Schlegel." *The Collected Works of Samuel Taylor Coleridge,* vol. 5, *Lectures 1808–19 on Literature,* ed. R. A. Foakes, 2 vols. (Princeton: Princeton Univ. Press, 1987), 1:lxii.

13. Arthur Eastman, *A Short History of Shakespearean Criticism* (New York: W. W. Norton, 1968), p. 70.

14. See Edward W. Tayler, *Donne's Idea of a Woman: Structure and Meaning in* The Anniversaries (New York: Columbia Univ. Press, 1991), pp. 20–67.

15. A. C. Bradley, *Shakespearean Tragedy* (1904; rpt. New York: Meridian Books, 1955), p. 98.

16. Norman Holland, *Psychoanalysis and Shakespeare* (New York: McGraw-Hill, 1966), pp. 163–206. A bibliography of psychoanalytic work on Shakespeare published after 1964, compiled by David Willbern, may be found in Schwartz and Kahn, *Representing Shakespeare.* The notes to the *Hamlet* chapter in Janet Adelman's *Suffocating Mothers: Fantasies of Maternal Origin in Shakespeare's Plays,* Hamlet *to* The Tempest (New York: Routledge, 1992) are impressively full.

17. Sigmund Freud, *The Origins of Psychoanalysis,* ed. Marie Bonaparte, Anna Freud, Ernst Kris (New York: Basic Books, 1954), p. 224. The person Hamlet has no trouble dispatching must be Polonius, not Laertes. The person to whom Hamlet transfers his stepfather's crime must be Gertrude, not Ophelia: "Almost as bad, good mother, / As kill a king and marry with his brother" (3.4.27–28). Both of the parapraxes—the first substituting a son for a father, the second a girlfriend for a mother—track back to the same moment in the play.

18. *The Standard Edition of the Complete Psychological Works of Sig-*

mund Freud, ed. James Strachey and Anna Freud, 24 vols. (London: Hogarth Press, 1953–64), 4:261–66.

19. Ernest Jones, "The Oedipus-Complex as an Explanation of Hamlet's Mystery: A Study in Motive," *American Journal of Psychology* 21 (1910): 72–113; Ernest Jones, *Hamlet and Oedipus* (New York: W. W. Norton, 1949).

20. Eliot's famous "Hamlet and His Problems" was first published in *The Sacred Wood* (London: Methuen, 1920), pp. 87–94. See the interesting remarks of C. L. Barber and Richard P. Wheeler in *The Whole Journey: Shakespeare's Power of Development* (Berkeley: Univ. of California Press), pp. 265–66.

21. A. C. Bradley, *Oxford Lectures on Poetry* (London: Macmillan, 1909), pp. 79, 77. Cf. George Brandes, *William Shakespeare* (1898; rpt. London: Heinemann, 1920), on *Hamlet*'s lacking "the lucidity of classical art; the hero's soul has all the untranspicuousness and complexity of a real soul" (p. 372), also p. 373: "In *Hamlet,* the first philosophical drama of the modern era, we meet for the first time the typical modern character."

This aspect of romanticism has of course many critics. One of the most influential, Irving Babbitt, complains that imagination is always associated with novelty, "which means, in the literary domain, with the expansive eagerness of a man to get his own uniqueness uttered" (*Rousseau and Romanticism* [Boston: Houghton Mifflin, 1919], p. 41).

22. Bradley, *Shakespearean Tragedy,* p. 108.

23. Lily Bess Campbell, *Shakespeare's Tragic Heroes: Slaves of Passion* (Cambridge: Cambridge Univ. Press, 1930).

24. Jacques Lacan, "Desire and the Interpretation of Desire in *Hamlet,*" trans. James Hulbert, *Yale French Studies* 55/56 (1977): 36–66.

25. Arthur Kirsch, *The Passions of Shakespeare's Tragic Heroes* (Charlottesville: Univ. of Virginia Press, 1990), p. 27.

26. J. O. Halliwell-Phillipps, *Memoranda on the Tragedy of Hamlet* (London, 1879), pp. 6–7.

27. Albert H. Tolman, "A View of the Views about *Hamlet,*" *PMLA* 12 (n.s. 6, 1898): 155–84.

28. Kuno Fischer, *Shakespeare's Hamlet* (Heidelberg, 1896); Lorenz Morsbach, *Der Weg zu Shakespeare und das Hamletdrama* (Halle a. S.,1922); Levin L. Schücking, *Character Problems in Shakespeare's Plays: A Guide to the Better Understanding of the Dramatist* (New York: Henry Holt, 1922). J. M. Robertson (whom T. S. Eliot had the cheek to agree with in "Hamlet and His Problems") may be sampled in *The State of*

Shakespeare Study: A Critical Conspectus (London: Routledge, 1931). E. E. Stoll wrote a great deal about *Hamlet*. A late summary statement may be found in *Art and Artifice in Shakespeare* (Cambridge: Cambridge Univ. Press, 1933), pp. 90–137.

29. L. C. Knights, *An Approach to 'Hamlet'* (London: Chatto & Windus, 1960), pp. 88–89.

30. A.J.A. Waldock, *Hamlet: A Study in Critical Method* (Cambridge: Cambridge Univ. Press, 1931), p. 30.

31. G. Wilson Knight, *The Wheel of Fire: Interpretations of Shakespearean Tragedy* (1930; rev. London: Methuen, 1949), p. 314.

32. All of the characters surrounding Hamlet have their defenders. Favorable views of Claudius can usually be traced to Howard Mumford Jones, "The King in *Hamlet,*" *University of Texas Bulletin* no. 1865 (Austin, 1918); an influential defense of Gertrude, exonerating her from the charge of adultery, is John W. Draper's "Queen Gertrude," *Revue anglo-américaine* 12 (1934): 20–34, later reworked in *The Hamlet of Shakespeare's Audience* (Durham: Duke Univ. Press, 1938).

33. A feebler version of this thesis may be found in Eleanor Prosser's *Hamlet and Revenge* (Stanford: Stanford Univ. Press, 1967).

34. John Dover Wilson, *What Happens in Hamlet* (Cambridge: Cambridge Univ. Press, 1935); *Hamlet,* ed. John Dover Wilson (Cambridge: Cambridge Univ. Press, 1934).

35. See also Robert H. West, *Shakespeare and the Outer Mystery* (Lexington: Univ. of Kentucky Press, 1968).

36. See also Jason Rosenblatt, "Aspects of the Incest Problem in *Hamlet,*" *Shakespeare Quarterly* 29 (1978): 349–64.

37. Roland Mushat Frye, *The Renaissance Hamlet: Issues and Responses in 1600* (Princeton: Princeton Univ. Press, 1984). Another and weaker book of this kind is Arthur McGee's *The Elizabethan Hamlet* (New Haven: Yale Univ. Press, 1987). A great deal of research, this time in the history of Renaissance drama, is said to prove that revenge is evil, the ghost a demon.

38. At least one of the resistance theorists (Bilson) distinguished between lineal and elected rulers, arguing that only the second could be resisted. Frye suggests that Hamlet's information about the Danish "election" comes late in the play, near the regicide itself, so that the original audience would understand the completeness of Hamlet's justification. But it is by no means clear that Danish kingship is *not* lineal; British monarchy was in a sense elective. See E.A.J. Honigmann's "The Politics in

Hamlet and 'The World of the Play'" in *Myriad-Minded Shakespeare* (New York: St. Martin's, 1989), pp. 43–59.

39. Fredson Bowers, *Elizabethan Revenge Tragedy* (Princeton: Princeton Univ. Press, 1940); "Hamlet as Scourge and Minister," *PMLA* 70 (1955): 740–49. For a brief critique of the essay, see the Jenkins *Hamlet,* p. 523. C. S. Lewis's "Hamlet: The Prince or the Poem?" (1942) is reprinted in *Interpretations of Shakespeare: British Academy Shakespeare Lectures,* ed. Kenneth Muir (New York: Oxford Univ. Press, 1986), pp. 124–41. Maynard Mack's "The World of *Hamlet,*" published in the *Yale Review* in 1952, may be found in Jump, Hamlet, *A Casebook,* pp. 86–107. Peter Alexander's ideas about the difference between the two Hamlets in *Hamlet: Father and Son* (Oxford: Clarendon Press, 1955) are endorsed by G. K. Hunter in *The Cambridge Companion to Shakespeare Studies,* ed. Stanley Wells (Cambridge: Cambridge Univ. Press, 1986), pp. 137–40; see also Paul Cantor's remarks on the contrast between father and son in *Hamlet* (Cambridge: Cambridge Univ. Press, 1989), pp. 32–40. Knights is cited in note 29, above. Patrick Crutwell's 1963 "The Morality of *Hamlet* — 'Sweet Prince' or 'Arrant Knave'" is also in Jump, pp. 174–95. For more on the criticism of this era, consult Randall E. Robinson, Hamlet *in the 1950s: An Annotated Bibliography* (New York: Garland, 1984).

Crutwell contends that efforts to find in the hero ethical scruples about revenge stem "from the very powerful quasi-pacifist emotions of many twentieth-century liberal intellectuals" (p. 184). In Prosser's *Hamlet and Revenge* the uneasiness has a Christian source, but the remark accurately describes Harold C. Goddard, *The Meaning of Shakespeare,* 2 vols. (Chicago: Univ. of Chicago Press, 1951), 1:331–86.

40. Harry Levin, *The Question of* Hamlet (Oxford: Oxford Univ. Press, 1959).

41. Margaret Ferguson, "*Hamlet:* Letters and Spirits," in Parker and Hartman, *Shakespeare and the Question of Theory,* p. 302.

42. Stephen Greenblatt, *Renaissance Self-Fashioning: From More to Shakespeare* (Chicago: Chicago Univ. Press, 1983), pp. 255–57. See also my "Individualism, Historicism, and New Styles of Overreaching," *Philosophy and Literature* 13 (1989): 115–26.

43. Stephen Greenblatt, *Shakespearean Negotiations: The Circulation of Social Energy in Renaissance England* (Berkeley: Univ. of California Press, 1988), pp. 1–3, vii.

44. Terry Eagleton, *William Shakespeare* (Oxford: Basil Blackwell, 1986), p. 72.

45. Harold Bloom, *Ruin the Sacred Truths: Poetry and Belief from the Bible to the Present* (Cambridge: Harvard Univ. Press, 1989), pp. 57–58. Hardin Craig, in "The Shackling of Accidents: A Study of Elizabethan Tragedy," *Philological Quarterly* 19 (1940): 1–19, also stresses the "indifference" of Hamlet in the final act, and goes so far as to paraphrase "We defy augury. There is special providence in the fall of a sparrow" as "I defy that augury which says that there is a special significance in the fall of a sparrow" (18). This peculiar interpretation skips right over providence, and annihilates the difference between Hamlet's two statements, of defiance and of providential trust, in one defiant indifference.

46. Schüking, *Character Problems in Shakespeare's Plays,* pp. 162–63.

47. *Hamlet,* pp. 149–53. See also Jenkins's extended discussion of the matter, "Hamlet and Ophelia," in Muir, *Interpretations of Shakespeare,* pp. 142–60.

CHAPTER 2. *Hamlet's* Good Night

1. It's getting hard to take. One of the television network anchormen, Peter Jennings, has begun signing off with "Have a nice evening."

2. Claude Lévi-Strauss, "The Sex of the Heavenly Bodies," in *Introduction to Structuralism,* ed. Michael Lane (New York: Basic Books, 1970), pp. 330–39.

3. Josua Poole, *The English Parnassus: Or, a Help to English Poesie* (London: Thomas Johnson, 1657), p. 142. A catalogue of the evils of night may also be found in Spenser's "Epithalamion," ll.315–52, in *Spenser's Minor Poems,* ed. Ernest de Sélincourt (Oxford: Clarendon Press, 1910), pp. 430–31. Clusters of nocturnal attributes are also common in the "farewell to the world" lyrics, such as Jonson's "False world, good night: since thou hast brought" in *Ben Jonson: The Complete Poems,* ed. George Parfitt (New Haven: Yale Univ. Press, 1975), p. 110, and the anonymous "Go, nightly cares, the enemy of rest" in *The Book of Elizabethan Verse,* ed. William Stanley Braithwaite (Boston: Herbert B. Turner, 1907), p. 503.

4. Stephen Batman, *The Golden Booke of the Leaden Goddes* (London, 1577), p. 27.

5. Milton mentions the association of night with grief in the Prolusion I am about to discuss. It is also crucial to the conceit of Donne's "A Nocturnall upon S. Lucies Day, being the shortest day": "Let mee prepare towards her, and let me call / This hour her Vigill, and her Eve, since this / Both the yeares, and the dayes deep midnight is." Part of the force

of "since" is that midnight, in this case the midnight of the day and the year, is the right time to mourn.

6. Campion's "Now winter nights enlarge" is quoted from Walter R. Davis, ed., *The Works of Thomas Campion* (New York: W. W. Norton, 1967), p. 147. The Donne passage may be found in W. Milgate, ed., *The Epithalamions, Anniversaries, and Epicedes of John Donne* (Oxford: Clarendon Press, 1978), p. 19; see also Abraham Cowley's "The Injoyment" in *Poems,* ed. A. R. Waller (Cambridge: Cambridge Univ. Press, 1903), p. 114. "Good night" has a sexual sense in James Shirley's "Good-night" in *Ben Jonson and the Cavalier Poets,* ed. Hugh MacLean (New York: W. W. Norton, 1974), p. 190.

Catalogues of the benign aspects of night are frequent in epithalamia; see for instance the "Epithalamion Teratos" in George Chapman's continuation of "Hero and Leander" in *The Works of Christopher Marlowe,* ed. C. R. Tucker Brooke (Oxford: Clarendon Press, 1910), pp. 541–42. A restful night, free of cares, often figures among the contentments in poems on the happy life; see Braithwaite, *The Book of Elizabethan Verse,* pp. 515–19.

7. *Paradise Lost* 3.45–47 in Merritt Y. Hughes, ed., *John Milton: Complete Poems and Major Prose* (New York: Odyssey, 1957), p. 259.

8. For "dead Season" see Frank Livingstone Huntley, *Bishop Joseph Hall and Protestant Meditation in Seventeenth-Century England* (Binghamton, N.Y.: Medieval and Renaissance Texts and Studies, 1981), p. 147.

9. Don M. Wolfe et al., eds., *The Complete Prose Works of John Milton,* 8 vols. (New Haven: Yale Univ. Press, 1953–82), 1:218–33. Milton concludes that prolonged night would mean the end of civilization and eventually human life, an idea explored in Isaac Asimov's "Nightfall," first published in *Astounding Science Fiction* in 1941 and reprinted frequently.

10. *Theogony* 123; also Sir Thomas Browne's *The Garden of Cyrus* in *Religio Medici and Other Works,* ed. L. C. Martin (Oxford: Oxford Univ. Press, 1964), p. 174.

Milton also knows the so-called Orphic hymns, an assembly of around ninety Greek poems of uncertain date passed down in a Byzantine collection. The "Hymn to Night," poem 3 in *Orphei Hymni,* ed. Gulielmus Quandt (Dublin: Weidmann, 1973), is a series of positive epithets for the goddess Night, source of everything. Raymond B. Waddington, in *The Mind's Empire: Myth and Form in George Chapman's Narrative Poems*

(Baltimore: Johns Hopkins Univ. Press, 1974), pp. 45–112, discusses the Orphic cult in Italian neoplatonism and its influence on Chapman.

11. On the proverbial idea of *Homo homini lupus* (Man is a wolf to man) see Kerrigan and Gordon Braden, *The Idea of the Renaissance* (Baltimore: Johns Hopkins Univ. Press, 1989), p. 38. Macbeth also identifies with night at 3.3.46–55. I am indebted throughout this chapter to Bradley's treatment (*Shakespearean Tragedy,* pp. 265–71) of the nocturnal atmosphere of *Macbeth.*

12. George R. Potter and Evelyn Simpson, eds., *The Sermons of John Donne,* 10 vols. (London: Univ. of California Press, 1953), 2:354–55. Hereafter the *Sermons* are cited in my text.

13. A parallel passage in Joseph Hall's *Occasional Meditations* may be found in Huntley, *Bishop Joseph Hall,* p. 134.

14. The conceit of life as a candle appears occasionally in lyrics; see Jonson's "On Spies" and Edward Herbert's "A Meditation upon his Wax-Candle burning out."

15. Fulke Greville, *Selected Poems,* ed. Thom Gunn (Chicago: Univ. of Chicago Press, 1968), p. 129.

16. Everything has been tried: S. Korner, "*Hamlet* as a Solar Myth," *Poet-Lore* 3 (1891): 214–16. Gilbert Murray stresses the battle between summer and winter in "Hamlet and Orestes: A Study of Traditional Types," *The British Academy Annual Shakespeare Lecture, 1914* (New York: Oxford Univ. Press, 1914). On the (slim) possibility that Shakespeare's "School of Night" in *Love's Labour's Lost* 4.3.214 names a contemporary cult of poets interested in skepticism and nocturnal symbolism, see Muriel C. Bradbrook's *The School of Night* (Cambridge: Cambridge Univ. Press, 1936).

17. On the backgrounds of the Pyrrhus speech in the Senecan tradition, see Else von Schaubert, "Die Stelle von Rauben Pyrrhus," *Anglia* 53 (1929): 374–439.

18. Interestingly, a comparable involvement with night is found in The Mousetrap's Lucianus:

> *Thoughts black, hands apt, drugs fit, and time agreeing,*
> *Confederate season, else no creature seeing,*
> *Thou mixture rank, of midnight weeds collected,*
> *With Hecate's magic and dire property*
> *On wholesome life usurps immediately.*
> > *Pours poison in the sleeper's ears.*

Some believe that this is the speech Hamlet inserts into The Mousetrap. In any case, the similarity of the nocturnal murderer to the nocturnal avenger is another instance of the doubling of Hamlet and Claudius.

19. The speech has either a source or a telling analogue in Thomas Kyd's *The Spanish Tragedy* 3.2.12–24, ed. T. W. Ross (Berkeley: Univ. of California Press, 1968).

20. See the OED entry for *soft* as an adverb, sense 8.

21. Gordon Braden, *Renaissance Tragedy and the Senecan Tradition: Anger's Privilege* (New Haven: Yale Univ. Press, 1968), pp. 219–20.

22. Maurice Charney comments on how the encounter with Claudius is made subordinate to Hamlet's appointment with Gertrude in "The 'Now I Could Drink Hot Blood' Soliloquy and the Middle of *Hamlet*," *Mosaic* 10 (1977): 77–86.

23. Cf. Fulke Greville, *Mustapha* 4.1.13–15: "What meanes that Glasse borne on those glorious wings, / Whose piercing shaddowes on my selfe reflect / Staines, which my vows against my children bring?" *Poems and Dramas of Fulke Greville,* ed. Geoffrey Bullough, 2 vols. (New York: Oxford Univ. Press, 1945), 2:110.

24. A similar interpretation of the ghost's second visit is found in Wilson, *What Happens in Hamlet,* pp. 172, 252. The classic discussion of matricide in the psychoanalytic tradition is Frederic Wertham's "The Matricidal Impulse: Critique of Freud's Interpretation of *Hamlet*," *Journal of Criminal Psychopathology* 2 (1941); 455–64.

25. Marcel Proust, *Remembrance of Things Past,* trans. Scott Moncrieff and Terence Kilmartin (New York: Random House, 1981), 1:13.

26. For a somewhat different view of the repeated "good night" in this scene, see Adelman's *Suffocating Mothers,* pp. 33–34.

27. On the comic in *Hamlet* see David Pirie, "*Hamlet* without the Prince," *Critical Quarterly* 14 (1972): 293–314, and Susan Snyder, *The Comic Matrix of Shakespeare's Tragedies* (Princeton: Princeton Univ. Press, 1979).

28. One would like to imagine that her interest in the names of flowers descends from Eve, who in *Paradise Lost* is given the privilege of naming flowers (11.277). To my knowledge, however, this is Milton's original touch, not a tradition.

29. See *The World runnes on wheeles: or, Oddes betwixt Carts and Coaches* in *All the Workes of John Taylor the Water Poet* (London: James Boler, 1630), pp. 232–44. Being a waterman whose trade was reduced by the coaches, Taylor was hardly an impartial observer.

30. 5.2.253–55 in Irving Ribner, ed., *The Complete Plays of Christopher Marlowe* (New York: Odyssey, 1963), p. 106.

31. The word *o'ercrows*, apparently derived from cockfighting, means "triumphs over," "belittles." See the citation in the Furness *Hamlet*, 1:453. Appropriately enough, Hamlet dies being reproached by the power of the poison.

32. A full set of Christian associations—sleep as death, the bed as the grave, "good night" as the promise of salvation—may also be found in "Gascoygnes good night" in *The Complete Works of George Gascoigne*, ed. John W. Cunliffe (Cambridge: Cambridge Univ. Press, 1907), 1:58–59.

CHAPTER 3. A Woman's a Two-Face

1. Knight, *The Wheel of Fire*, p. 21.

2. It is perhaps worth knowing that Thomas Hill's *The Contemptation of Mankind* (London, 1571) urged a revival of physiognomy; see Carroll Camden, "The Mind's Construction in the Face," *PQ* 20 (1941): 400–412.

3. An entire genre of the lyric, the so-called "complaint," is given over to this situation. Shakespeare's "A Lover's Complaint" is an apt example.

4. See Kerrigan and Braden, *The Idea of the Renaissance*, pp. 136–40.

5. Robert Burton, *The Anatomy of Melancholy*, ed. Floyd Dell and Paul Jordan-Smith (New York: Tudor, 1927), p. 759.

6. Jacob Burckhardt's discussion of cosmetics in *The Civilization of the Renaissance in Italy*, trans. S.G.C. Middlemore, 2 vols. (New York: Harper & Row, 1958), 2:363–66, cites literary examples of condemnation; Ariosto's fifth satire is particularly savage on the practice. Admittedly, neither Jonson's "Still to be neat" nor Herrick's "Delight in Disorder" praises cosmetics. Edward William Tayler cites Herrick's "Painting sometimes permitted" in *Nature and Art in Renaissance Literature* (New York: Columbia Univ. Press, 1964), pp. 14 ff. Although there are Cavalier examples of this praise, I do not know of any Elizabethan ones. The best-known instance in English verse is Pope's tribute to "the cosmetic powers" in *The Rape of the Lock*, 1.121–48; he may have been influenced by Mary Evelyn's *Mundus Muliebris: or, the Ladies Dressing-Room unlock'd, and her Toilette Spread* (1690), which can be sampled in *Kissing the Rod: An Anthology of Seventeenth-Century Women's Verse*, ed. Germaine Greer et al. (New York: Noonday Press, 1989), pp. 325–28. Another poet in this volume, the anonymous author of *Triumphs of Female Wit* (1683), contrasts cosmetic and literary adornment in a way

that concedes their similarity: "Our Minds, and not our Faces, we'll adorn" (*Kissing the Rod,* p. 312). Poetry against cosmetics takes its inspiration from Ovid's *Remedia Amoris* 351–56, though his fragmentary *Medicamina Faciei Feminae* recommends beauty treatments for the female face. George Turbervile attacks the face-painting of an aged woman in "Leave off good Beroe now" but does not condemn the practice itself (*The Works of the English Poets,* ed. Samuel Johnson, 21 vols. [London: J. Johnson and others, 1810], 2:622). On Shakespeare's unrelieved disdain for cosmetics, see Edward A. Armstrong's *Shakespeare's Imagination* (Lincoln: Univ. of Nebraska Press, 1982), pp. 66–71.

7. The quotations are, in order, from Anthony Munday, *A Second and Third Blast of Retrait from Plaies and Theaters* (London, 1580), p. 145, and Stephen Gosson, *Plays Confuted in Fiue Actions* (London, n.d.), pp. 165, 197. On the duplicity of players see also Phillip Stubbes, *The Anatomie of Abuses* (London, 1583), p. 140: "beware, therefore, you masking players, you painted sepulchres, you double dealing ambodexters."

8. *The Poetry and Prose of William Blake,* ed. David V. Erdman (Garden City, N.Y.: Doubleday, 1970), p. 465.

9. On the relationship of these ideas to Renaissance love poetry, see Kerrigan and Braden, *The Idea of the Renaissance,* pp. 188–89, and Kerrigan and Gordon Braden, "Milton's Coy Eve: *Paradise Lost* and Renaissance Love Poetry," *ELH* 53 (1986): 27–51.

10. The classic statement is in Ernest Jones, *Hamlet and Oedipus,* p. 86.

11. Ernest Jones, *Hamlet and Oedipus,* pp. 88–91.

12. Peter Erickson, *Patriarchal Structures in Shakespeare's Drama* (Berkeley: Univ. of California Press, 1985), p. 186.

13. For infantile fantasies about choking and smothering in Shakespeare, see Alan Rothenberg, "Infantile Fantasies in Shakespearean Metaphor: (1) The Fear of Being Smothered," *Psychoanalytic Review* 60 (1973): 205–22, and "The Oral Rape Fantasy and Rejection of the Mother in the Imagery of Shakespeare's *Venus and Adonis,*" *Psychoanalytic Quarterly* 40 (1971): 447–68. Rothenberg does not suggest an etiology for this complex of fantasies in Shakespeare.

14. "Too much of a good thing is wonderful," as Mae West remarked.

15. Kerrigan, *The Sacred Complex: On the Psychogenesis of Paradise Lost* (Cambridge: Harvard Univ. Press, 1981), p. 162.

16. To my knowledge the prevalence of hendiadys in *Hamlet, Troilus and Cressida,* and *Measure for Measure* was first noticed by Rossiter (*Angel with Horns,* pp. 163–64). George Wright's wittily titled "Hendia-

dys and *Hamlet*," *PMLA* 96 (1981): 168–93, is superb on the poetic effects of the device but eventually loses touch with the play in its devotion to rigorous classification. Frank Kermode widens the discussion to doubles of all kinds in *Forms of Attention* (London: University of Chicago Press, 1985), pp. 35–63. Ted Hughes brilliantly returns to the level of poetic technique in *Shakespeare and the Goddess of Complete Being* (New York: Farrar, Straus & Giroux, 1992), pp. 129–42.

17. I guess I have not shown *all* my cards. I also believe that women to some degree collude with men in maintaining versions of the split. Female coyness, which is not found in classical literature, is an example of female sexuality negotiating with the male split. It plays with sending contrary signals: I am above sexual interest, I am sexually interested.

18. The two best guides to the subject are Ann Jennalie Cook's "'Bargains of Incontinencie': Bawdy Behavior in the Playhouses," in *Shakespeare Survey* 10, ed. J. Leeds Barroll III (New York: Burt Franklin, 1977), pp. 271–90, and in the same volume, Wallace Shug's "Prostitution in Shakespeare's London," pp. 291–313. E. J. Burford's *Bawds and Lodgings: A History of the Bankside Brothels ca. 1000–1675* is lively but not always reliable.

19. I have used the edition of the play in *The Chief Elizabethan Dramatists,* ed. William Allan Neilson (Boston: Riverside, 1911).

20. Huntley, *Bishop Joseph Hall,* p. 173.

21. In the "Execration Upon Vulcan" Jonson punningly blames the whore Kate Arden for "burning" (giving the pox to) the Globe Theater (141–44), then at the end of the poem returns the curse in a curse: "Thy wife's pox on thee, and Bess Braughton's too" (216).

22. Eliot, in this sense, is correct: the language hurled by Hamlet toward Gertrude and her recent marriage is indeed in excess of the facts. But the excess is generic. In this period, brothel language creeps into indictments of female immorality no matter what the offense. Probably the place to start on Renaissance attitudes toward women is Louis B. Wright's *Middle-Class Culture in Elizabethan England* (Ithaca: Cornell Univ. Press, 1958). Carroll Camden's *The Elizabethan Woman* (Houston: Elsevier, 1952) and Linda Woodbridge's *Women and the English Renaissance: Literature and the Nature of Womankind, 1540–1620* (Urbana: Univ. of Illinois Press, 1986) are also excellent and contain helpful bibliographies.

23. *Epigrammes* 83.

24. *Honest Whore,* Part 1, 1.5.48–49.

25. On the general subject see Curtis Brown Watson, *Shakespeare and*

the Renaissance Concept of Honor (Princeton: Princeton Univ. Press, 1960). His work is criticized in Paul N. Siegel, *Shakespeare in His Time and Ours* (Notre Dame: Univ. of Notre Dame Press, 1968), pp. 122–62. There is also material on honor scattered here and there in James C. Bulman, *The Heroic Idiom of Shakespearean Tragedy* (Newark: Univ. of Delaware Press, 1985). For a reading of *Hamlet* based on conceptions of honor, see Martin Dodsworth, *Hamlet Closely Observed* (London: Athlone, 1985). The second-best discussion I know is Gordon Braden, *Renaissance Tragedy and the Senecan Tradition,* pp. 73–86, and the best, Burckhardt, *The Civilization of the Renaissance in Italy,* 2:426–43. For Burckhardt honor is "that enigmatic mixture of conscience and egotism" (p. 428).

26. Ralegh has honor as reputation in mind in "The Lie" ("Tell honour how it alters"), and so too does Falstaff: "But will it not live with the living? No? Why? Detraction will not suffer it" (*1H4* 5.2.138–40). Attacks on honor in this sense may be found in Girolamo Cardano, *Cardanus Comforte* (London: Thomas Marsh, 1576), pp. 95–96, and Samuel Purchas, *Microcosmus, or the Historie of Man* (London: Henry Fetherstone, 1619), pp. 457–72. Except now and then in military contexts, Montaigne has little use for honor or glory; see *Complete Essays,* pp. 468, 595–96. Henry Cornelius Agrippa's disdain for honor in *The Vanity of Arts and Sciences* (London: R. Everingham, 1694), pp. 257, 273, is part of his general contempt for nobility.

For its defenders, however, honor is a concept between the individual and society. On one side it is fame or reputation, while on the other it is conscience or self-esteem, often with a familial inflection. Thus Ralegh, in another mood in *The History of the World,* ed. C. A. Patrides (Philadelphia: Temple Univ. Press, 1971), p. 65: "honour is left posterity for a mark and ensign of the virtue and understanding of their ancestors." See also Peter de la Primaudaye, *The French Academie* (London: George Bishop, 1589), pp. 234, 243–44.

27. See Watson, *Shakespeare and the Renaissance Concept of Honor,* pp. 437–47. On the gender difference at issue here, see Keith Thomas, "The Double Standard," *JHI* 20 (1954): 195–216.

28. *The Poems of Thomas Carew,* ed. Rhodes Dunlap (Oxford: Clarendon Press, 1949), p. 49. See also Donne's "Communitie" and "Confined Love." For more detail on honor and Renaissance poetry consult Kerrigan and Braden, *The Idea of the Renaissance,* pp. 171–79.

29. "Feminine Honour" in Dunlap, *The Poems of Thomas Carew,* pp. 60–61.

30. The twins in *The Comedy of Errors* and *Twelfth Night* indicate a fascination with same and different. One also thinks of "The Phoenix and the Turtle." Edward Tayler writes brilliantly about division and negation in "*King Lear* and Negation," *ELR* 20 (1990): 17–39.

31. Elizabeth Freund, "'Ariachne's broken woof': The Rhetoric of Citation in *Troilus and Cressida,*" in Parker and Hartman, *Shakespeare and the Question of Theory,* pp. 19–36.

32. I want to acknowledge my general indebtedness to A. P. Rossiter's treatment of *Troilus* in *Angel with Horns,* pp. 129–42; I never felt I understood the play until reading this essay. But for Rossiter, the play leads toward a general relativism and perspectivism (134–36). What's aught but as 'tis valued? Everyone has their "Helen" and their "Cressida." In my view, however, intrinsic virtue has not been banished from the sphere of love: Cressida becomes for Troilus, and through him for the future, a standard of intrinsic falsehood: the woman who will disillusion a man. Graham Bradshaw's discussion in *Shakespeare's Skepticism* is also insightful, particularly his opening remarks about the Prologue (127), but it seems a bit much to praise Achilles for his brisk practicality in the killing of Hector (138–39).

CHAPTER 4. Hamlet's Virgin

1. John Donne, "Twicknam Garden," ll. 8–9.

2. Wilson, *What Happens in Hamlet,* p. 306.

3. Dante places suicides in the second ring of the seventh circle of Hell (*Inferno* XIII).

4. It is not difficult to pluck from Hamlet's list of the ills we bear one destined to figure in his exchange with Ophelia: "The pangs of dispriz'd love" (3.1.72).

5. Cf. *As You Like It* 1.2.36–38.

6. For John Ford in *Honor Triumphant* (1606) it was still a paradox: "Now so much difference is there, betwixt the wanton and the *faire,* as the wanton may be beloved, but the *faire,* wil not be wanton." He goes on to quote the proverb that has gone sour for Hamlet: "*rara proeclara:* according to the proverbe, that the *fairest* are the *fairest,* that is the best and best to be esteemed." I quote from *The Nondramatic Works of John Ford,* ed. L. E. Stock et al. (Binghamton, N.Y.: Medieval and Renais-

sance Texts and Studies, in conjunction with the Renaissance English Text Society, 1991), pp. 44–45.

7. On "yes" and "no" in primitive splitting see Freud, "Negation," in *The Standard Edition,* 19:235–42, and René A. Spitz, *No and Yes: On the Genesis of Human Communication* (New York: International Universities Press, 1956).

8. See the OED entry for *Go,* 91, also 34 and 35.

9. Linda Woodbridge writes of the close affinity between misogyny and humor in *Women and the English Renaissance,* pp. 31, 318–19.

10. Jenkins, p. 294. On the motif of the hero lying in a woman's lap see Mary Nyquist's "Textual Overlapping and Dalilah's Harlot-Lap" in *Literary Theory/Renaissance Texts,* ed. Patricia Parker and David Quint (Baltimore: Johns Hopkins Univ. Press, 1986), pp. 341–72.

11. Adelman, *Suffocating Mothers,* p. 12.

12. See the Jenkins note on "blister," p. 321.

13. J. V. Cunningham's remarks on this phrase, and the speech it concludes, are suggestive; see *The Collected Essays of J. V. Cunningham* (Chicago: Swallow, 1976), pp. 100–102. He observes that Hamlet treats commonplace sins as if they were impossible, the result being an expression of moral horror.

14. As Sidney writes in *An Apology for Poetry,* "to fall lower, the *Terentian Gnato* and our *Chaucers Pandar* so exprest that we nowe vse their names to signifie their trades." *Elizabethan Critical Essays,* ed. Gregory Smith, 2 vols. (London: Oxford Univ. Press, 1904), 1:166.

15. Knights, *An Approach to 'Hamlet',* p. 65.

16. Furness, *Hamlet,* 2, p. 77 (ll. 1756–57).

17. The subject of the ballad is no doubt traditional. See "My love hath vowed" in Davis, *The Works of Thomas Campion,* p. 27.

18. For a feminine analysis of this male double bind see Aphra Behn's "*To* Alexis *in Answer to his Poem against Fruition*" in Greer et al., *Kissing the Rod,* pp. 258–59.

19. J. V. Cunningham puts it well: "The problem here involves a choice between no action, rational action with a view to consequences, and action at any cost. The contrast between the latter two resembles that between the chivalric rashness of Hotspur and the staid courage of Prince Hal. In this case it is solved in favor of Hotspur" (*Collected Essays,* p. 118). With Hamlet's submission to rash action, "The play whose plot had displayed the scheme of moral action ends with the renunciation of it" (119).

20. Adelman, *Suffocating Mothers,* pp. 34–35.

CHAPTER 5. The Last Mystery

1. Kerri Thomsen has suggested to me that Hamlet's allusion to his father's "sepulchre" having opened "ponderous and marble jaws" (1.4.48, 50) implies burial in a crypt, perhaps in Elsinore's chapel. But calling the ghost a "mole" working in the "earth" (1.5.170) suggests burial in the graveyard.

2. Furness, *Hamlet,* 1:383. The edition is that of Charles and Mary Cowden Clarke.

3. Shakespeare's epitaph, quite possibly authentic, comes to mind here. Peter Levi calls it a "conversation with gravediggers" in *The Life and Times of William Shakespeare* (New York: Holt, 1988), p. 343.

4. On the double as "uncanny harbinger of death," see Freud, *Standard Edition,* 17:235.

5. Montaigne, "Of the resemblance of children to fathers," in *Complete Essays,* p. 578.

6. Freud, *Standard Edition,* 4:261, 7:195, 9:135. See also Géza Roheim, *The Riddle of the Sphinx,* trans. R. Money-Kyrle (New York: Harper, 1974), pp. 1–9.

7. The full text of the poem is given in Furness *Hamlet,* 1:381.

8. *Habington's Castara,* ed. Charles A. Elton (Bristol: J. M. Gutch, n.d.), p. 151. The scene may have a classical source in Lucian's *Dialogues of the Dead* 5–6 in *Lucian,* vol. 7, trans. M. D. MacLeod (London: Heinemann, 1961). Much like Hamlet, Menippus joins with death in verbally taunting the skulls of Homer's heroes. Alexander later (25) appears as a character.

9. There are of course many great Renaissance poems inspired by this ancient theme. See especially George Herbert's "Church Monuments" in *The Works of George Herbert,* ed. F. E. Hutchinson (Oxford: Clarendon Press, 1941), p. 64.

10. Walter N. King, *Hamlet's Search for Meaning* (Athens: Univ. of Georgia Press, 1982), pp. 140–41.

11. K. R. Eissler, *Discourse on Hamlet and* Hamlet: *A Psychoanalytic Inquiry* (New York: International Universities Press, 1971), pp. 84–85.

12. Cf. *Measure for Measure* 3.1.19–21: "Thou art not thyself / For thou exists on many a thousand grains / That issue out of dust."

13. I discuss the new restlessness in Renaissance representations of death in "On the Deaths of Individualism" in *Taking Chances: Derrida,*

Psychoanalysis, and Literature, ed. Joseph H. Smith and William Kerrigan (Baltimore: Johns Hopkins Univ. Press, 1984), pp. 88–103.

14. Seneca's *Thyestes,* 195–96; the line is quoted by the ghost of a murdered father to instruct his son in John Marston's *Antonio's Revenge* 3.1.51, ed. G. K. Hunter (Lincoln: Regents Renaissance Drama Series, 1965). I use the translation of Gordon Braden in *The Legacy of Rome: A New Appraisal,* ed. Richard Jenkyns (Oxford: Oxford Univ. Press, 1992), p. 258. My thoughts here are very close to those of Paul Gottschalk, "Hamlet and the Scanning of Revenge," *Shakespeare Quarterly* 24 (1973): 155–70, who also quotes this line from Seneca.

15. Look for him under your boot soles. It almost goes without saying that Hamlet's reflections bear no hint of Whitman's pantheistic atomism, where dissolution into the grass licenses expansive democratic egotism. There may be just a touch of early modern ecological harmony; a bung-hole needs stopping, after all, and something must do the job. But the dominant note is greatness rebuked, egotism's comeuppance. These are "base uses."

16. Rom. 12.19: "Dearly beloved, avenge not yourselves, but rather give place unto wrath: for it is written, Vengeance *is* mine; I will repay, saith the Lord."

17. Braden, *Renaissance Tragedy and the Senecan Tradition,* p. 203. I am indebted throughout the second half of this chapter to Braden's richly suggestive discussion of the genre and *Hamlet*'s place in it.

18. Paul Cantor, for example, thinks "the tragic conflict between the classical and Christian elements in Hamlet" is ultimately incapable of resolution (*Hamlet,* p. 63). Yet what we call Christianity is itself in some measure an accommodation with classical culture. Earlier, Cantor notes in the play a "new emphasis on the mysterious depths of human interiority that goes hand in hand with the Christian concern for the salvation of souls" (p. 45). It seems to me that Hamlet does achieve, in the new interiority of Act 5, a vision of his situation in the world that is both Christian and vengeful.

19. A great deal of information about skulls and the *memento mori* tradition can be found in Frye, *The Renaissance Hamlet,* pp. 206–43. Hall contrasts the classical with the Christian meaning of the skull in Huntley, *Bishop Joseph Hall,* p. 182.

20. Fredson Bowers argues that Shakespeare has Christianized the classical "moment of final suspense" in *Hamlet as Minister and Scourge and*

Other Studies in Shakespeare and Milton (Charlottesville: Univ. Press of Virginia, 1989), pp. 114–22.

21. *Institutes* 1.16.3 in *Calvin: Institutes of the Christian Religion,* ed. John T. McNeill, trans. Ford Lewis Battles, 2 vols. (Philadelphia: Westminster Press, 1960), 1:202. Jenkins directs us to *Institutes* 1.16.1 and 1.17.6 where Matt. 10.29 is cited in connection with special providence. Although Calvin distinguishes providence from stoic fate, it is interesting that his first book was a commentary on Seneca.

22. Ernest Jones, *Hamlet and Oedipus,* p. 99.

23. Frye, *The Renaissance Hamlet,* p. 268, aptly quotes *Macbeth* 1.7.10–11: "This even handed justice / Commends th' ingredience of our poisoned chalice / To our own lips."

24. Barber and Wheeler, *The Whole Journey,* p. 264, note that revenge commonly involves a representation of the crime (an eye for an eye), and cite work in progress by David Willbern.

25. "Father and mother is man and wife, man and wife is one flesh" (4.4.54–55).

26. On "matter" and *mater* in *Hamlet* see Margaret Ferguson in Parker and Hartman, *Shakespeare and the Question of Theory,* pp. 294–96.

Index

Designed by Martha Farlow

Composed by A. W. Bennett, Inc., in Sabon with display in Phaistos

Printed by Thomson-Shore, Inc., on 50-lb. Glatfelter Supple Opaque and bound in Holliston Crown Linen